THE NEW RULES OF EQ

USING EMOTIONAL INTELLIGENCE TO GET AHEAD

Rob Yeung

Marshall Cavendish
Business

Copyright © 2006 Rob Yeung

First published as The Rules of EQ in 2006.
This edition published in 2012 by Marshall Cavendish Business
An imprint of Marshall Cavendish International

1 New Industrial Road, Singapore 536196
genrefsales@sg.marshallcavendish.com
www.marshallcavendish.com/genref

Other Marshall Cavendish offices: Marshall Cavendish Corporation. 99 White Plains
Road, Tarrytown NY 10591-9001, USA • Marshall Cavendish International (Thailand)
Co Ltd. 253 Asoke, 12th Flr, Sukhumvit 21 Road, Klongtoey Nua, Wattana, Bangkok
10110, Thailand • Marshall Cavendish (Malaysia) Sdn Bhd. Times Subang, Lot 46,
Subang Hi-Tech Industrial Park, Batu Tiga, 40000 Shah Alam, Selangor Darul Ehsan,
Malaysia

Marshall Cavendish is a trademark of Times Publishing Limited

The right of Patrick Forsyth to be identified as the author of this work has been asserted
by him in accordance with the Copyright, Designs and Patents Act 1988.

A CIP record for this book is available from the British Library

ISBN 978-981-4382-30-4

Printed in Singapore by Fabulous Printers Pte Ltd

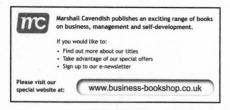

Marshall Cavendish publishes an exciting range of books
on business, management and self-development.

If you would like to:

- Find out more about our titles
- Take advantage of our special offers
- Sign up to our e-newsletter

Please visit our
special website at: www.business-bookshop.co.uk

Contents

Foreword

Working life ain't simple any more. There was a time when you worked hard, your employer looked after you, and you just carried on until you received your golden carriage clock on retirement. But that simple career path is dead. There are more threats in the world – mergers and acquisitions, globalization and jobs being outsourced or offshored, downsizing programs, and job cuts. And these have turned the workplace into a minefield of treacherous personalities, unexploded resentments, and ticking egos. Who can you really trust? What do you need to do or say to get ahead?

But there are more opportunities too. You aren't tied to just one employer any more – you can move around and look for bigger pay rises, more interesting challenges, and greater responsibility. Employers no longer look down on people who want to take career breaks to go traveling or do something different. You could go freelance or set up your own business and try to make your first million. The world is your oyster.

In this complex world of work, the rules of work have changed. We can all think of people who got promoted who didn't deserve to be. Come to think of it, we can all probably think of people who do deserve to get promoted, but haven't been. But the good news is that emotional intelligence is well established as the single biggest contributor to making a success of yourself.

These days it is no longer the most intelligent people in the classical sense – individuals with skyscraper-high IQ scores – who succeed in the world. There are plenty of "clever" or "bright" people who never make it. Some of them have great ideas but don't have the motivation to do anything about them. And then there are the ones who have not succeeded because they lack social skills – they are rocket scientists or "geeks."

Instead, the people who succeed often have fairly modest ideas – but are good at motivating themselves and influencing others. When average people feel angry, they lash out. Or when they feel unhappy, they stop working. But emotionally intelligent people understand their own moods and how to motivate themselves despite feeling angry or unhappy. And when they need to influence others, they can cajole and persuade others to help them out.

Managing your own emotions and those of others plays a huge part in who succeeds. Anyone can become more successful by paying attention to the skills of emotional intelligence – and this book shows you how.

But let's cut to the chase. After all, who has the time to sit and read hefty management tomes? Too often, an author has a handful of great ideas, but then ruins them by spending hundreds and hundreds of pages explaining them carefully in excruciating detail, giving too much background and yawn, yawn, yawn ... readers lose the will to live.

When I read one of those books, I start to flick through the chapters and pages with increasing impatience – wanting to shout, "Come on, get to the point!" Ah, but there is a reason that those books are so long. The truth of the matter is that many publishers want their authors to write lengthy books so that they can then slap on a big fat cover price.

This book you hold in your hands will not patronize or talk down to you. It is not a guide for idiots or dummies. You are a bright professional who simply wants some new ideas on how to develop your emotional intelligence by mastering your own moods and emotions and those of others. You do not need everything spelt out for you with endless examples to get the point across – although I have chosen a small number of examples (usually having changed the names to protect the guilty) to illustrate key points.

So if you have ever wanted to know how to get ahead in your career – but don't have the time to plough through Bible-sized manuals or books that talk down to you – then this is the book for you. Feel free to flick through and find the chapters that are most interesting for you.

Drop me an email if you have any thoughts or observations about emotional intelligence.

Rob Yeung
rob@talentspace.co.uk

01

Introduction

WHAT IS EMOTIONAL INTELLIGENCE EXACTLY?

Unless you are a recent arrival on our planet, you will have heard of emotional intelligence. However, there is still a lot of misunderstanding about what it actually describes.

In one sentence, emotional intelligence is the ability to identify, understand, and manage moods and feelings – in both ourselves and other people.

But a single sentence doesn't really help us to understand why emotional intelligence is useful. Breaking it down further gives us three domains of expertise:

- *Self-awareness.* The first step in becoming emotionally intelligent is to be able to identify moods and feelings in ourselves and understand how these affect other people. Many people are blind to the true impact that they have on others. We like to think of our own strengths and weaknesses in one way – but others often have a very different idea of how they would describe us.

- *Self-direction.* Identifying our own emotions and how they affect people is a start, but the second step to becoming emotionally intelligent is to alter those emotions and set goals to your advantage. Because often the only difference that distinguishes winners from losers is their mental state. Knowing that you are angry or tired and unhappy isn't very helpful. But being able to change your mood to one of calm or enthusiasm – now, that's a worthwhile skill.

- *Interpersonal savvy.* The third step to becoming a master of emotional intelligence is to identify and manage emotional states in other people. In today's world, people don't have to do something just because you tell them to. Even if you are the boss, they can choose to do it more slowly or to put less energy into it if they choose. So interpersonal savvy is the skill of finding out what makes other people tick so that you can influence and persuade them. A cynic might describe it as the dark art of pushing other people's buttons and manipulating them to achieve your goals.

The three domains of expertise are hierarchical – they build into a pyramid with self-awareness being the foundation for the other two. The next layer is being able to self-direct – to alter your moods and emotions on demand. But at the top of the pyramid is the expertise of interpersonal savvy – being able to identify and manage emotions not only in yourself but also in other people.

When you have mastered interpersonal savvy, there may still be challenges that you feel you cannot overcome. And that is where organizational savvy comes in – the application of the three skills of emotional intelligence to tackling teams and organization-wide problems and opportunities.

The three domains of self-awareness, selfdirection, and interpersonal savvy, plus their application as organizational savvy, mirror the four major parts of the book. I imagine that many readers will be tempted to skip ahead to read about how to influence and persuade the people around you. If you want to do it, then do it. But you won't be as effective at influencing others until you have learnt to analyze and understand emotions and control them in yourself. So make sure that you return to the earlier parts on selfawareness and self-direction to round off your emotional intelligence.

A CONDENSED HISTORY

If you want a treatise on the history of emotional intelligence, look elsewhere. You don't need to know the history in order to become emotionally intelligent. But having a few key facts at your disposal will help to shut up the smart-asses in the world who seem to exist for the sole purpose of showing off their knowledge of trivia.

Psychologist Daniel Goleman started the trend off in 1995 when he published a book called simply Emotional Intelligence. It was an instant bestseller. Translation into 30 languages and sales of several millions, as well as a followup book, *Working with Emotional Intelligence*, have secured Goleman's status as the adopting father of emotional intelligence and helped to make the term a permanent addition to the language of the workplace.

While Goleman is the adopting father, the biological father of emotional intelligence remains in doubt. Perhaps the kudos should go to the psychologist with the wonderful name of Orval Hobart Mowrer, who originally coined the phrase back in 1960. Or maybe the credit should to go two other psychologists, Peter Salovey and John Mayer, who conducted much of the research that Goleman later went on to recycle in his best-selling book.

At the end of the day, it's not important to us. Let's focus instead on why emotional intelligence should be of interest to you – how you can develop it to further your personal goals.

WHY BOTHER WITH EMOTIONAL INTELLIGENCE?

Here's the secret. What Goleman, and Salovey and Mayer, and hundreds of other academics, business school professors, and managers agree on is that emotional intelligence is hugely important for success at work. I could bore you by quoting hundreds of research articles to back up this claim, but I won't.

Traditional intelligence – or a high IQ score – has never been enough to succeed. The kids we grew up with who excelled at school exams aren't always the ones who are having the greatest careers. Plus there are plenty of people who never went to university – or didn't even finish school – but went on to set up their own businesses and who are doing very nicely for themselves indeed.

Emotionally intelligent individuals are able to identify what they feel and intentionally generate other mood states to help them achieve their goals. In other words, they know how to motivate themselves. And motivation is often the biggest difference between success and failure, between being a winner and an also-ran. Many entrepreneurs and business leaders are no smarter than we are, but they succeed because they set a goal and pursue it with dogged determination. When they suffer setbacks and feel despondent, they are able to lift their own mood and get on with the work at hand. Even if they feel incredibly nervous before a big presentation, they have learnt to calm themselves and project an aura of confidence. When they are faced with obstructive people, they know when to hold their temper in check and when to lose it. They are aware of their own emotions and able to manage them.

Interpersonal skills form another important component of emotional intelligence. Consider where you work and the various people you come into contact with through work. Who is the best manager in your organization? What is it that they do that makes them a good manager? Are they good because they are smart and clever? Or good because they are charming and supportive, charismatic and enthusiastic?

I would hazard a guess that it is the latter case. We may respect people who are clever, insightful, and sharp. But we like the ones who are positive and socially skilled. And, more often than not, we go out of our way to help people who we like rather than the ones we respect.

So unless you work in a sealed room with no contact with other people, being able to identify what makes other people tick will help you to gain support from others and be more effective. Becoming emotionally intelligent allows you to identify when you might need to cajole, criticize, command, compliment, and compromise – and how to do it well.

And, best of all, emotional intelligence is a skill that anyone can improve with a bit of patience and effort.

DO IT FOR YOU

Organizations are fascinated by emotional intelligence because to them it is a way of developing employees to work more productively. They want you to work harder – they want to get more out of you.

But let's look at it from another perspective. Rather than thinking of emotional intelligence as a tool for helping the organization, think of it as a tool for helping you to achieve your own personal goals. Whether you want to climb the career ladder or set up your own business, negotiate a better work–life balance, or learn how to handle difficult colleagues, becoming more emotionally intelligent can help.

Let's face it – if your organization needed to make 15 percent of its workforce redundant, do you think executives would have any qualms about letting you go? Or if they could replace you with a cheaper alternative – a computer or a call center operative in India – do you think that they would hesitate for even one moment?

And don't expect your boss to look after you. I promise there won't be too much research in this book, but this one made me smile. Just this year, Belinda Board and Katarina Fritzon published research measuring psychopathic personality traits in a sample of senior managers and chief executives, plus a group of patients currently incarcerated in a mental institution. Guess what? The managers came out scoring higher on narcissistic, histrionic, and compulsive personality traits than the patients. So if your boss is lacking in empathy, superficially charming, and perfectionist, who's going to look after your interests?

Yes, there may be a greater good for the organization in developing your emotional intelligence. But this book is about helping you to succeed. Forget about being a good team player for a change and think about playing in your own team of one. The organization can look after itself; let's look after you for a change.

PRACTICE MAKES PERFECT

Do you remember how it felt when you were first learning to drive? I'm guessing that you stalled the car more than a couple of times. And you were almost certainly either driving too fast or too slow – or both at different times. Your instructor probably had to wrest control of the steering wheel away from you a couple of times too to avoid a head-on collision.

But that's no surprise whenever you learn a new skill.

Before you had started driving, you probably thought that it looked quite easy. Until we start learning any new skill, we don't realize how bad we really are at it – to use a piece of jargon, we are "unconscious about our incompetence."

But as you drove the car a bit more, you became more confident about it. You learnt to find the bite point on the clutch and to check the mirror before maneuvering. But you still had to think about what you needed to do. You were able to drive – but it required considerable conscious effort on your part. You became "consciously competent."

As you spent more and more time driving, your confidence grew. And now you can drive without having to think about it. You don't think about how you drive – you just do it. You can admire the scenery and not worry about what your feet and hands are doing anymore because your brain and body have become "unconsciously competent." Your competence is now an automatic part of you.

Those stages are the same for the learning of any new skill – including emotional intelligence. At first most people are unconsciously incompetent – completely unaware of how bad they are at it. As you read the book and try some of the skills, you may learn some techniques very quickly but be frustrated by others – but you will develop your skills and become consciously competent. One day in the future, you will cease to think about the techniques because you will be using them automatically. They will have become part of your natural habit. It takes a lot of practice to get to this point of "unconscious competence," but it can be done.

02

Self-Awareness

We're all good with some skills and not so good with others. Thinking about myself, I've been told that I communicate well – I give engaging presentations and write in jargon-free English. However, I know that numbers are not my strong suit and I would much rather leave spreadsheets and financial analysis to other people.

But in my heart of hearts, I also know that I sometimes delude myself about my weaknesses. I like to think that I'm better at business development than I probably am. And I'm not very good at hiding my impatience with people despite my best efforts.

It is human nature to allow ourselves to exaggerate our strengths and disregard our weaknesses. We all do it to some degree. However, emotionally intelligent people do it very little while the emotionally ignorant do it a lot.

The first step to becoming emotionally intelligent is to become as self-aware as possible. We all experience emotions, but for the most part, we simply allow those emotions to happen – we don't scrutinize them and evaluate whether they are helping us or hindering us.

Becoming self-aware also applies to becoming aware of the impact that you have on other people. You may believe that you have certain strengths and weaknesses – but your beliefs may hinder your goals if other people feel that you actually have very different strengths and weaknesses.

Once you become aware of your own emotions, strengths, and weaknesses, you can begin to think about how to manage and apply them to help you achieve your goals. When you are feeling down, you can lift your mood to get on with whatever you need to do. But what are your goals? Do you want more money and a bigger office? Do you want to be the boss or your boss's boss? Or do you have ambitions of making a contribution to society? Unless you are aware of what your goals are, why you want them, and how you are going to achieve them, you will not reach them.

Becoming self-aware is like the first step of a meeting at Alcoholics Anonymous. I've never been to one, but I've watched enough television dramas to get the picture. It's always a heartrending moment when the hero or heroine puts up a hand and says, "I am an alcoholic." Being aware of the problem and recognizing it is the first step to getting over alcoholism.

The same is true with your emotions. Recognizing that you experience emotions is a first step to wielding them effectively. Recognizing the impact that you have on the emotions of other people is a vital step to influencing them effectively. And identifying your goals will help you to achieve them.

UNDERSTAND THE BRAIN–BODY–BEHAVIOR CONNECTION

Psychologists are wonderful people – and I'm not just saying it because I'm a psychologist – because they have established time and again that there is an inextricable link between the brain, the body, and our behavior.

What we think and feel, how our bodies react, and how we behave are linked. If we think that an important presentation is going to be a disaster, then we feel nervous; our hearts may pound and our breathing quicken. The combination of emotional feelings and physical sensations makes us likely to make a mess of it. But if we think that it is going to go well, then we feel confident; our heart rate and breathing remain normal. And it helps us to deliver an effervescent performance.

Thoughts lead to feelings and physical sensations. Feelings and physical sensations shape our behavior. And, in turn, behavior affects our thinking.

More importantly, positive thoughts lead to positive feelings and stable physical sensations. Positive feelings lead to successful behavior. And successful behavior leads to more positive thinking.

Psychologists use this chain of events in the treatment of clinical depression. When patients fall into a funk, psychologists use cognitive-behavioral therapy (CBT) to retrain their behavior and thoughts, which lifts their mood. If they are unhappy, then behaving as if they are happy can actually alleviate their mood – even in clinically depressed patients.

I'm not suggesting years of therapy. But you can apply the principles to your own emotions to help you to succeed.

We'll come back to this brain–body–behavior notion later. For now, let's get on with some action.

EXAMINE YOUR EMOTIONS

The first time I had to give a presentation to a client, I thought my heart was going to explode. I was in my early twenties and had started working for the Boston Consulting Group, a large management consultancy. I had been gathering data for months and was presenting my findings to a handful of managers – the youngest of whom was at least 15 years older than I was. And a few of them had been in the industry for longer than I had been alive. Nervous? No, I was terrified.

In retrospect, there was nothing to be afraid of. I had done my research. I had written my slides and rehearsed what I was going to say. But I still felt terrified.

And the big problem is that we experience emotions without really considering whether they are appropriate or not.

We all experience emotions. And when we experience emotions, it is easy to let them affect our behavior. If we feel nervous going into a crucial sales meeting, we are probably going to fail to impress the customer. If we feel miserable before going to a party, we won't want to talk to people – and that will just reinforce our feelings of unhappiness.

The key to ultimately controlling your emotions is to be more aware of them and to examine them. Rather than letting them happen to you, think through why you are experiencing particular emotions.

Every time you feel yourself experiencing an emotion – whether it is sadness or fear, anger or exhilaration – take a few minutes to examine it as objectively as you can. In practice, doing it every time you experience an emotion would leave you no time to do anything else – so just do it as often as you can. Pick different situations, interactions, and encounters so that you can analyze and examine different emotions.

The key to examining your emotions is to identify the thoughts that led to the emotions that you experienced. We all have an inner voice that evaluates what is going on around us. From the moment we wake, our voice speaks to us: "Oh no I have that interview today. I don't know why I'm bothering, as I'll never get it."

Our self-talk then causes us to experience emotions and physical sensations such as butterflies in the stomach. But our self-talk often does not describe the reality of a situation. If you have been invited to an interview, then you probably have as good a chance of getting the job as any other candidate. It is only because your self-talk is negative that causes you to feel overly anxious.

If you can identify what you are thinking, then you will eventually be able to retrain your thoughts in a more positive and productive direction. But for now, let's focus on examining your emotions and the thoughts that led up to them.

Whenever you can, ask yourself the following questions:

- What emotion did I experience? (If you struggle to

identify the precise emotion or feeling that you were experiencing, then take a look at the list in the next section – "Label your emotions").

- What physical sensations did I experience? Think of a racing heart, sweaty palms, quickening of the breath and so on.
- What were the thoughts that were going through my head at the time?
- Was the emotion appropriate or inappropriate? Was it helpful or hindering me from doing what I wanted to do?

Going back to the example of waking up and thinking that you'll never pass an interview, you may have experienced anxiety coupled with feelings of physical, muscular tension and a tight feeling in your stomach. You may have been thinking that this interview will not be successful because you have not been for an interview in several years. For now, this realization is enough. In the next part, we shall discuss how to challenge the negative thoughts that may pop into your head.

Some people find it useful to keep a mood log – a diary into which they write about events and the associated emotions and thoughts that accompanied them. It may sound like a trite exercise, but most people – even quite senior and experienced managers – find that it helps them to analyze events in a more productive light. Over the course of months, it also allows you to identify whether there are particular patterns to the emotions that you experience, which will help you to find practical ways to break negative patterns and reinforce positive ones.

Don't just pick bad events and negative emotions. Practice examining some successes and positive emotions too, as it will help you to develop more fully your ability to scrutinize emotions. If you can understand what causes positive emotions, then you will eventually be able to generate them on demand.

LABEL YOUR EMOTIONS

Even though I'm a psychologist, I still find it difficult to describe in precise terms what I am feeling. Most of the time, I just know that I'm feeling bad or good. The precise label or adjective doesn't always come to me.

But the path to self-awareness requires that you are able to identify different feelings, moods, emotions, and other mental states as accurately as you can.

Overleaf is a list of useful words to help you along the way:

Table 1		
Excited	Dejected	Outraged
Proud	Cheerful	Scared
Helpless	Trapped	Relieved
Confident	Disappointed	Relaxed
Depressed	Powerful	Afraid
Appreciated	Upset	Furious
Fulfilled	Enthusiastic	Panicky
Happy	Pleased	Insecure

Ecstatic	Unhappy	Annoyed
Abandoned	Competent	Incompetent
Hurt	Aggressive	Apprehensive
Sluggish	Cheerful	Terrified
Crushed	Nervous	Remorseful
Unsure	Embarrassed	Shy
Elated	Unappreciated	Miserable
Jealous	Frustrated	Distressed
Disgusted	Anxious	Desperate
Lonely	Irritated	Contented
Overwhelmed	Bored	Ashamed
Insecure	Surprised	Patronized
Hopeless	Puzzled	Sad
Calm	Unworthy	

Make a mental note of this page and refer back to it frequently.

DISTINGUISH BETWEEN FACT AND FEELING

There's a scene in the Woody Allen film *Annie Hall* when the main character and his girlfriend go to see a counselor because they are experiencing difficulties in their relationship. The counselor asks them, "How often do you have sex?" The Woody character replies, "Hardly ever – three times a week." And his girlfriend replies, "All the time – three times a week."

Even though different people may experience the facts around an event in the same way, they may interpret them in different ways. And interpreting them in different ways will lead to different feelings.

At work, let's consider how often a customer service manager picks up the telephone to speak to customers. One customer might feel constantly pestered by two phone calls a month, while another might feel neglected by the same number of calls. The fact is that the manager is making two calls a month. But it elicits very different feelings in each customer.

Training yourself to distinguish between fact and feeling will further enhance your selfawareness.

The only facts that exist are what you pick up through your five senses – seeing, hearing, touching, smelling, and tasting. Everything else is either a thought or a feeling.

Let's take a more practical example. "She was rude to me" is an evaluation – a thought that might elicit a feeling, perhaps of hurt or anger. The facts of the situation might be that your colleague raised her voice and said, "Listen, I don't have the time for this – can I call you back?" before hanging up the telephone. And then maybe the fact that she never called back elicited a feeling. But rudeness is an interpretation. What you interpreted as rudeness, another person might have interpreted as being busy and then forgetting to call. Certainly, you can't know what was going on in your colleague's head.

Here is another example: you have been asked to give a presentation to a prospective client. Afterwards, you might think, "He was unhappy with the presentation" – but that too is another evaluation. The facts might have been that the client frowned while raising three queries about the presentation. But if you don't know the client well enough, perhaps you don't appreciate that he always frowns when he is concentrating. And how do you know that he doesn't raise many more queries when listening to other presentations?

Learning to distinguish between the facts and your interpretation/feelings will help you to become more actively aware of your emotions as a precursor to controlling them.

MARRY YOUR PERCEPTIONS WITH THOSE OF OTHERS

I once worked at a consulting firm for a boss (John) who proudly described himself as forthright, uncompromising, and persistent. But when the company fell upon hard times, he tried to become even more forthright, more uncompromising, and more persistent – not only with clients but also with the team. It didn't work. Because while John thought he was being more forthright, uncompromising, and persistent, the rest of us thought he was becoming tactless, inflexible, and dogmatic. So the talented consultants left and took the few remaining clients with them.

There is often a big difference in how we choose to think about ourselves and how others feel about us.

It happened to me once too. When I joined the same consulting firm, I thought that I was a confident person who was good at taking charge in ambiguous situations. I was more than a little shocked when a colleague told me that the rest of the team thought I was a bit arrogant. And could I stop being quite so bossy please?

When it comes to strengths and weaknesses, there is no absolute reality. It is all a matter of perception. And, often, what we perceive to be our greatest strength – the skill that we are proudest of – is exactly what others perceive to be our greatest weakness. The reverse can be true too – sometimes we think we aren't very good at something when others may see it as a real strength of ours.

A vital step in becoming emotionally intelligent is to think about how your behavior may impact on others.

Here's an exercise for you. Take a few moments to think of a handful of adjectives that you feel happy to use in describing yourself. It could be five adjectives or it could be a dozen. The precise number doesn't matter. But do take a moment to think about it. Perhaps jot them in the margin of the book.

OK, now look at the following list of adjectives. Do any of your adjectives appear in the left-hand side of the list? If so, the right-hand adjective is how you could be coming across to people.

Ambitious	Ruthless
Assertive	Bullying
Caring	Meddlesome
Cautious	Indecisive
Confident	Arrogant
Enthusiastic	Overzealous
Extroverted	Loud
Fun	Frivolous
Honest	Tactless

Helpful	Interfering
Honorable	Moralistic
Independent	Isolated
Loyal	Servile
Persistent	Dogmatic
Practical	Unimaginative
Realistic	Pessimistic
Restrained	Introverted
Spontaneous	Disorganized
Supportive	Compliant
Thorough	Obsessive
Tolerant	Uncaring
Tough	Callous
Trusting	Gullible

The list isn't meant to be comprehensive, but you're a smart individual and you get the point. Just because you like to see yourself in one light does not mean that others will always agree with you.

REFLECT AND EVALUATE

This is an exercise in self-analysis. Take time out to give greater consideration to whether your strengths could manifest themselves as weaknesses in the eyes of other people. Take each of the adjectives you chose and try to recall occasions when you behaved in that way. For example, if you believe that you are loyal, when did you last demonstrate your loyalty? Or if, at the moment, you believe that one of your major strengths is that you are confident, then what concrete examples can you recall to support that belief?

The acronym SABRE may help you to analyze the events that come to mind:

- Situation – what was the situation?
- Action – what actions did you take? What emotions did you display?
- Behavior – how did others behave? How did they respond to you and any others that might have been involved? What emotions did they show?
- Result – what happened as a result of your actions and their behavior? What was the outcome and what emotions did it leave everyone with?
- Evaluation – looking back on the whole event and evaluating it, what could you have done differently (i.e. better)?

Some people like to take notes to help them evaluate events properly. Even if you can only set aside 10 to 20 minutes a week to start with, try it to improve your ability to critique your own behavior and emotional life.

Reflection and evaluation is a powerful tool in becoming emotionally intelligent. But boosting your emotional intelligence does not happen overnight. Yes, there are some tools and tips that will help you to manage yourself and other people almost immediately, but learning any worthwhile skill takes time and effort. Learning to play the piano, you don't get to play Rachmaninov straight away. Picking up tennis, you would not expect to serve 100 mile an hour aces immediately. So don't expect to become an expert at deploying the varied skills of emotional intelligence without some work and practice on your part either.

SEEK FEEDBACK

The list of adjectives can highlight potential mismatches between how you like to describe yourself and how other people might really see you. It is a useful exercise to start you off on the road toward becoming fully self-aware.

However, the only way to find out what others really think of you is to ask them. And there is nothing like talking to them to find out how they really feel about you.

Begin by considering who might be able to provide you with some feedback. If you are trying to improve your effectiveness at work, pick colleagues and suppliers, clients, and other contacts. If you don't work with your friends and family, don't pick them.

You could start by emailing them to warn that you will call. Then make sure that you do call.

The questions don't have to be terribly complicated – just a few simple questions:

- What are my strengths? What do I do or say that makes me effective?
- What are my weaknesses? Can you think of any examples of times when I have annoyed you or been ineffective?
- What could I be doing differently? Do you have any suggestions for how I could be more effective?

In listening to them, pay attention not only to what they say, but also how they say it. They might say, "I can't think of anything that you dowrong." But was there an uncomfortable pause before they said it? Does the tone of their voice sound sincere?

And don't let them off the hook immediately. Keep probing. Ask your questions in different ways to help them give you useful pointers. Emphasize that no one is perfect and that the feedback will really help your personal development. If they have identified three strengths for you, encourage them to identify three weaknesses to balance out the feedback.

When you have obtained the feedback, reflect on it. Are there any patterns? What else does it tell you about the person that others see you as?

ACCEPT FEEDBACK WITH GOOD GRACE

Last year, a client organization of mine started a 360° feedback program to get managers and staff to comment anonymously on each other's performance. Each manager received feedback from their boss, a couple of peers, and most of their direct reports. Afterwards, the HR director told me that one of the managers – on having received comments that were not to his liking – dragged each member of his team into his office to ask them who had said what about him.

When they repeat the 360° feedback program this year, do you think that his team is going to risk saying anything even remotely negative about him again?

It is natural to feel surprised, shocked, or disappointed – and hopefully sometimes even delighted – by unexpected feedback. Whenever I gather feedback on myself, there is always something that I was not expecting – and not usually in a good way. But if you want to learn from feedback (and ever want people to give you candid feedback again), you need to respond to feedback in the right way.

You must thank people and show your gratitude for the time and effort they have put into thinking about your strengths and weaknesses. No matter how much you might disagree with their comments, you must appreciate that people are entitled to their perceptions. Don't get defensive. Don't try to justify it. Just thank them for their comments. Accept that when it comes to interpreting feelings and emotions, there are no absolutes. In working on your emotional intelligence, it is more important to become aware that your behavior can and does affect people in different ways.

IDENTIFY YOUR PRIORITIES

There's not a lot that separates the people who succeed from those who don't. But one of them is having a vision or some aims in life. Most people stumble through their lives, too busy worrying about their day-to-day existence to think about what could make them happier. Do you know what is important to you? Do you know what you want to get out of life and your work?

More on vision later. But for now let's spend a little time thinking about your priorities in work and life. Becoming more aware of them will help you to achieve them – if you don't know what you want, how can you strive for it?

The following is a list of priorities that you may or may not be looking for – in both your work and life outside of work:

Influence	Challenge	Learning
Travel	Friends	Health
Spiritual growth	Contribution to society	Personal growth
Creativity	Friendship	Fun
Risk	Freedom	Security
Respect	Structure	Autonomy
Predictability	Excitement	Responsibility
Appreciation from others	Family	Geographical location
Equity ownership	Leisure time	Predictable working hours
Loving partner	Personal possessions	Wealth
Children	Status	Stability
Competition	Achievement	Loyalty
Control	Income	Set up own business

Your task is to take the list and put the priorities in rank order of importance to you. Put the most important priorities at the top and the least at the bottom of the list. The best way of doing this is to write each priority out on a fresh Post-It note, and to keep rearranging the list until you are satisfied with the ordering.

You are not allowed to have any tied rankings. Life is often about making trade-offs. There are only 24 hours in the day and much as we might like to do it all, the reality is that we can't. If you want to pursue financial success, are you willing to sacrifice your leisure time? If you want risk and excitement in your job, how compatible is it with having a family and children?

But feel free to add further priorities to the list. If there is something that is of particular importance to you, do include it.

Once you are happy with the ordering of your list, you should have a better idea of what drives you in your life. Being more aware of your priorities will allow you to make clearer decisions and trade off between different options and opportunities in order to reduce stress and increase your satisfaction with your work and life.

WRITE YOUR EULOGY

Imagine that you are dead – 30, 40, or 70 years into the future – and picture a gathering of friends and family, colleagues, and acquaintances mourning by the side of your coffin. Your best friend begins to read the eulogy. What would you want him or her to say?

It is a cliché to say that no one on their deathbed ever wished they had worked harder. So use this exercise as an opportunity to ask yourself: How would I like to be remembered?

This is an extension of the priorities exercise and is designed to help you clarify further a vision of what you want from your life. Give yourself at least a half hour and take a clean sheet of paper to begin:

- Write a detailed description of how you would like a close friend to describe you at your own funeral. It doesn't matter if you write it in prose or in bullet points – this is not an essay that you ever need share with anyone else.

- Think about both your professional and personal life. Refer back to your list from the priorities exercise too. If you want to be remembered as a great leader, then what would that leadership role look like?

- Don't forget to include all of the social relationships you have – with family, friends, community groups, and so on. What are the key relationships in your life? And how important are they in relation to your work? For example, I have met more than a few executives who claim that their families are the most important priorities in their lives – but if that were really true, then why do they work 16-hour days and spend so much time away from home? Society sometimes conditions us to say that certain things are important. But this exercise is about identifying what is really important to you – so don't include priorities because you think you need to. Include them only if you want to.

- Bear in mind that this is how you would like to be remembered. Don't allow your eulogy to be bogged down by the current reality of your life. This is an opportunity to enhance your awareness of goals and aspirations that you have yet to realize.

- On the other hand, keep your eulogy realistic. Yes, you may want to win the lottery and be remembered for living a playboy lifestyle. But how likely is that? Finding a new job or retraining in a new career, moving to a new country, or setting up your own business – those are probably more reasonable.

Many people are hesitant to embark on the eulogy exercise. In fact, I'd say that most people I've asked to write a eulogy have been more than a little skeptical. But what do you have to lose by giving it a go? No one else ever needs to see it. You probably spend more time watching television every week than it takes to write a eulogy. And it is a fantastic tool for identifying a clear vision for your career and life. Guaranteed. If you do it properly and it doesn't work for you, write to me and complain.

Many people like to draft a version, put it away and reflect, and return to it again and again over the course of several days or weeks. A few people can write the entire eulogy in one sitting. Do whatever works for you.

DISCOVER YOUR VISION

Remember that developing a vision is about helping you to differentiate yourself from the rest of the crowd who wander aimlessly through life. If you ask them how they are doing, they reply that "things aren't bad" or that they are "getting by." They are mired in coping with their day-to-day lives, not thinking about what they want out of the future. Unless you want to be one of the floundering masses, take the time to identify your vision.

A vision is a dream of what success looks like, an idea of what people want to achieve with their lives. Only by knowing what success looks like are people able to achieve it. Successful people don't believe in luck – they create their own success by having a vision. They dare to dream and then turn it into reality through persistence and self-motivation.

The priorities and eulogy exercises should have given you an indication of what is important to you. Now it is time to bring them together in discovering your own vision. What would success look like to you?

A vision need neither be worthy in the eyes of other people nor huge and unwieldy. Yes, some people do want to cure cancer or put an end to wars, hunger, and poverty. But your own vision needs only be important and worth achieving to you. You might want to build a million-pound business in five years or become chief executive by the time you are 50. Perhaps you want to prioritize above all other things becoming a good parent and seeing your children fulfill their own potential. Or maybe you want to travel the world or be an author and write the book that you have been talking about.

Make sure that your vision is phrased positively – about what you do want to do – rather than about what you don't want to do or need to avoid.

Find some quiet time to ask yourself:

- What do I hope to achieve? What are my goals in life? Think about both personal and career goals and the balance you wish to strike between the two.
- Are my goals stretching, but within the bounds of possibility? A vision is of no use if it is completely and hopelessly unattainable.
- What would success feel like? Imagine that you have achieved your goals. What emotions would you feel?

The acid test of whether your statements form the basis for a true vision is to ask yourself how you would feel if you were to fail to achieve it. Well, how would you feel? If the answer is that you wouldn't be too bothered – then it's not a proper vision. A vision needs to engage your emotions. It is not a mere action plan of tasks that you want to achieve. It should sum up your life's ambitions. If you don't feel strongly about wanting to achieve it, then it's not right for you. Keep trying until you come up with something that you feel passionate about.

SET SMART GOALS

I know I said that this book wouldn't be full of research, but bear with me just this once, OK?

Back in the 1950s, researchers asked a bunch of Harvard University graduates about their goals. As you might expect, almost all of them had goals. But only 3 percent of them actually wrote them down. Fast-forward 30 years to a follow- up survey. And guess what? The researchers found that those 3 percent had amassed as much wealth as the other 97 percent put together.

Have I got your attention yet? Tempted to write any goals down?

Your vision provides you with a picture of where you want to be. But translating it into a set of more specific goals will help to vault you into that top 3 percent. Yes, I know there is more to life than money. And money doesn't buy happiness. But it can buy a nice home and a lot of holidays while you try to figure out what might make you happy!

If you have ever been sent on a pesky management development course, you will have been introduced to the concept of devising SMART goals. But rather than using it to get a project done more quickly at work, try applying it to your own vision:

- **S**pecific – your goal needs to be precise, not woolly. Not just "I want to be promoted" – promoted to what exactly? But "I want to be a marketing director."
- **M**easurable – whether you reach your goal or not has to be quantifiable. It has to be as black and white as possible. If others cannot agree categorically "yes" or "no" that a goal has either been reached or not, then it's not measurable enough. "I want to run a successful business" – how? In what way? "I want to run a £10 million business with a 20 percent profit margin" – that's more like it.
- **A**chievable – the goal needs to be stretching, but attainable. "I want to build a profitable business

that will take people to another galaxy" is probably a little too stretching. But "I want to build a profitable business that will fly people from London to LA in eight hours" – might debatably be achievable in our lifetime.

- **R**ealistic – the goal also needs to be realistic for you. Don't compare yourself with the wrong people. Yes, the Olympic record holder may be able to run the marathon in just over two hours. But given the constraints in your life, is it really realistic to expect that you will be able to train for eight hours a day, six days a week? Keep it real.

- **T**imed – your goal needs a deadline. "I want to quadruple the size of the business." Is that by next Wednesday or in five years' time? If you do not set a sensible timescale to the goal, the danger is that it may be impossibly stretching or simply too far in the future to worry about. If you don't need to start on it for another ten years, it's not going to motivate you to do anything about it today is it?

Keep that wealthy 3 percent of the Harvard boys and girls in mind. And now go and write out your SMART goals.

03

Self-Direction

If emotional intelligence were a journey, then selfawareness would be the skill of map reading. It tells you where you are at the moment – the current mood or emotion you may be experiencing. And it shows you where you want to get to – a goal, or perhaps an emotion or mood that may help you to achieve your goal. But it doesn't allow you to get from one to the other.

For instance, being aware that you are in a foul mood is a start. And you probably know that you would rather be in a good mood. But knowing how to move from one to the other is another matter.

And that is where the skills of self-direction come into play. Learning to self-direct will allow you to find the right path and clamber over obstacles that may block your way. If one road is blocked, self-direction is the skill that will help you to find another route.

I've said it before and I'll say it again. Successful people are usually no cleverer than we are. What they are better at is motivating themselves when they feel despondent.

They feel worried and afraid but decide to do it anyway. When they lack confidence, they find ways to summon up courage. They get embarrassed and angry too, but they hide it and get on with the task at hand.

I came across one such fellow recently. I was waiting in the reception of a big law firm when a uniformed gentleman asked me if he could polish my shoes. It was a free service that the law firm was paying for. We chatted while he cleaned – he asked me what I did for a living and, out of politeness, I asked him how he had got into the shoe cleaning business. He explained that he had left school without many qualifications and decided to polish shoes for a living. He set up a stand and cleaned people's shoes every morning. And every afternoon he knocked on big companies' doors and asked if they would like someone to polish shoes for them. Most declined. But he kept trying for months and months. And then a big bank said "Yes." So he cleaned shoes for the bank and hired someone to tend his original stand. He knocked on more doors and other people said "yes" too.

He didn't tell me exactly how much he earns, but he now has more than a dozen people working for him, all polishing shoes in swanky establishments. And he now only works part-time because he enjoys chatting to new people.

I bet that there were days when he was tired and unhappy. I'm sure some people will have laughed in his face at his idea. But he kept his motivation high and kept knocking on doors.

Let's help you to knock on some doors too.

BREAK THE LINK

Suppose that you have just finished working with the project from hell. Over-budget but underdelivering, the unhappy team is now reviewing the many problems that happened along the way. Suddenly a colleague singles you out for blame, saying that it's all your fault and that if you had paid more attention, it would have worked out fine.

How would you feel? Perhaps shocked, hurt, and angry.

As your heart pounds and your breath grows short, you counter that he was equally to blame. Within seconds, voices are raised and the meeting is a washout. Everyone comes away feeling bruised, friendships are broken, and the team is never quite the same again.

But it doesn't have to happen that way.

Normally, our thoughts lead us to experience feelings and physical sensations. And together, our thoughts, feelings, and physical sensations determine how we behave. But when we feel threatened, our emotions bypass conscious thought. We literally act first and think later. Often, we act first and regret later.

It's an evolutionary response that used to save us from being eaten by saber-toothed tigers. When you saw a giant cat pouncing on you, it was safer to run first and ponder later.

In modern life, we're not usually in danger of being eaten. But unfortunately our bodies still want to respond to the same evolutionary response.

Thankfully, we can break the link by choosing not to act first and think later. The moment you feel any emotions and accompanying physical sensations, you need to question them. Ask yourself what you are feeling.

When that colleague shouts at you, don't just let the emotions and physical sensations take control of you. Give the emotion a name. I'm feeling angry now. And identify the physical sensations. My heart is racing and my palms are getting sweaty. I can also feel a vein pumping in my right temple.

It takes willpower to stop yourself from reacting. But if you can stop yourself for even a moment to name the emotions you feel and list your physical sensations, you will give yourself a chance to break the link between emotion and action.

And once you have broken that link, three further techniques will help you to exert complete control over your emotions:

- Challenging automatic negative thoughts;.
- Putting it into perspective.
- Managing physical sensations and symptoms.

Let's look at each of these in turn.

CHALLENGE AUTOMATIC NEGATIVE THOUGHTS

When a situation goes wrong, we might think: "I'm giving the worst presentation ever. How embarrassing – I wish I could curl up and die. I might as well give up now." Or when we feel angry with someone, we may be thinking: "I could kill him now. I could punch him in the face – I don't care if I get fired."

These "automatic negative thoughts" (ANTs) are private, uncensored views that pop into our heads whenever we experience strong emotions. Challenging them is a key to controlling our emotions and channeling them more productively.

Our ANTs often voice our negative feelings about other people at that moment – "bastard," "I wish she would fall under a bus," or "I wish everyone would just piss off." Sometimes we refer to ourselves in a negative fashion – "I am so screwed," "I'm going to lose my job for this," "I look stupid in front of everyone."

It's not wrong to have these ANTs – we can't help having dark thoughts occasionally – but it is usually unhelpful to act upon them. Most of the time, we realize that we can't curl up and die or punch someone in the face. But our ANTs can still influence our behavior – we might metaphorically curl up and die by being rendered too nervous to speak clearly, or might lash out with a cutting remark and a string of expletives rather than with our fists.

Challenging our ANTs can help us to consciously choose how we want to behave, rather than letting those automatic thoughts lead to automatic actions that we might later regret. We can choose. In that presentation, we can make ourselves continue regardless of the mistakes we might have made; when feeling angry we can decide to seek a more productive way to resolve the situation.

I know a manager who scribbles in his notebook the phrase "Look out for ANTs!!!" at the start of meetings.

But it helps to remind himself to look out for them and challenge them when he finds them crossing his mind.

Whenever you hear those dark thoughts – your ANTs – crawling into your consciousness, challenge them. Begin by acknowledging that you are experiencing an ANT. If you hear your inner voice threaten someone or hear your self-talk make a negative claim about yourself, say to yourself "that's an ANT" or "I am experiencing an automatic negative thought." The mere act of labeling it will help you to impose some control over your emotions.

Then challenge the ANT. Is the ANT helpful? Is it even true? Going on to question the nature of your ANTs will stop them from influencing your behavior.

PUT IT INTO PERSPECTIVE

A colleague of mine once lost a big client. When the phone call came through that the client was dumping us, Jane took it hard. She burst into tears and, between sobs, muttered that it was her fault, it was a disaster, and that she was going to lose her job.

I didn't know whether it was her fault or not. And maybe it felt like a disaster to her, but it wasn't a disaster to the company as we had other, bigger clients. And I knew for a fact that she was still one of our best business developers, so was definitely not going to lose her job.

We are all guilty of over-generalizing at times. "I'm never going to get a new job," "He is always late for meetings," "She never listens to me." But the truth of the matter is that these over-generalizations are rarely true. Yes, you may have failed at another interview – but you will probably get another job. It will just take more time and hard work. He may often be late for meetings, but is he late for every single one, 100 percent of the time? And while a colleague may not have paid attention to you several times, she probably listens to at least some of what you say – although perhaps not to the more important advice that you give her.

Over-generalized statements are another form of automatic negative thoughts. So the important knack is to monitor and challenge them. "I'm being attacked by an ANT. Is it helpful? (No). Is it true? (No)."

Another useful tactic if you feel that an issue or problem is generating unhelpful ANTs and emotions is to scale it down. Ask yourself the following:

- Is the problem going to kill anyone?
- Will the problem still be affecting me in five years' time?

The answer to both of those questions is almost always "No." And the very act of measuring the impact of any particular problem on your life will help you to keep it in perspective.

MANAGE PHYSICAL SENSATIONS AND SYMPTOMS

How do you feel when you're afraid, tense, or angry? Ever get trembling hands, sweaty armpits, a racing heart, sticky palms, a dry throat, quickening breath, a headache, tight muscles? Physical sensations and symptoms go hand in hand with strong emotions. It's part of that evolutionary response that saved us from being turned into a saber-toothed tiger's dinner. When we feel threatened, our brains prep our bodies for "fight or flight" by tensing muscles and pumping blood and oxygen to vital organs – to get ready to thump the predator or run from it.

Thankfully, the link between our brains and our bodies is a two-way street. Yes, our emotions can cause physical sensations. But by controlling our physical sensations we can further control unhelpful emotions.

Let's take a couple of examples.

When you feel panicky, your muscles may involuntarily bunch up with tension. But if you pay attention to the tension in your shoulders and force them to loosen, you will help to drive the panic away. If you feel your jaw setting and your teeth grinding, relax your jaw and force yourself to smile.

Or how about when you feel your palms getting sweaty? Try to make your way to a sink and run them under a cold tap. Rinsing the sweat away will help to calm your nerves.

Our breathing often changes when we feel anxious too. We tend to pant, taking quick, shallow breaths into the tops of our lungs. But forcing yourself to breathe more slowly and deeply into your lower lungs – your diaphragm – can make you feel calmer.

Most people find the technique of diaphragmatic breathing the most useful but also the most difficult to master. Practicing it when you are relaxed will enable you to muster it up whenever you need to feel calmer.

One of the easiest ways to learn how to do it properly

is by experiencing its opposite first. Begin by lying on a flat surface. Place your right hand on your chest and your left hand on your belly button. Now take fast, short breaths, concentrating on expanding only your chest area – your right hand rising and falling while your left hand stays static. After 20 or 30 breaths, you will feel dizzy – because shallow breathing makes you feel anxious.

Now try diaphragmatic breathing by taking long, slow breaths into your belly. Your left hand should rise and fall, while your right hand stays still. When you get it right, your fingers and toes should tingle as your body relaxes and returns blood from your vital organs to your extremities. You should feel relaxed to the point of nearly falling asleep.

Anyway, that's enough of physical sensations. Paying attention to them and modifying them alongside of challenging ANTs will help you to feel calmer.

RECITE PERSONAL AFFIRMATIONS

It doesn't take a Nobel Prize winner to tell you that the more you think glum thoughts, the more you feel unhappy. Negative thoughts trigger negative emotions. But the two-way street that is the body–brain–behavior link allows us to manipulate our emotions by training our brains to engage in positive thoughts.

The previous three techniques were about breaking the link between unhelpful thoughts and emotions. But this one is about taking positive steps to preempt that cycle from starting in the first place.

Personal affirmations are constructive statements about

yourself. The act of reciting positive comments about yourself will enable you to manipulate your mood. For example, if you are feeling jittery before a key meeting, you might recite to yourself: "I am confident. I have done my preparation and I'll make a good job of it." But you must do it with conviction. Repeating it once or twice will hardly make a difference. You need to pay attention to the words – make your inner voice as loud as possible and stress the important words.

Even better, try to say your personal affirmations out loud. The combination of saying them and hearing your own voice makes for a more powerful mood booster.

Personal affirmations should always be phrased positively – about what you want to achieve – rather than negatively about what you want to avoid. For example, "I am calm and confident" rather than "I am not nervous."

The best way to use personal affirmations is to prepare them in advance for the stressful event. For example, if you are worried about your appraisal, you might prepare: "I have worked hard over the last year. I will impress my boss." Or if you need to confront someone, you might prepare: "I will stay calm and ask questions to understand her point of view."

But to be really effective, your personal affirmations need to be relevant to you and your situation. Taking affirmations from this book or even from someone else will do you little benefit. Try it now. Have a think about the next stressful situation that you need to face. What are the two or three personal affirmations that you could repeat then?

A lot of my coaching clients are reluctant to try personal affirmations. Some think that the idea sounds a bit outlandish. Others believe that they are above such petty tactics. A few are worried that they might get laughed at. But who says that you have to do it in public? And the truth is that more successful people use the technique than you realize. It's a secret that works – most people who use it would rather keep it to themselves. Affirmations work.

I know a chief executive in the television industry who speaks out loud his personal affirmations before major presentations and difficult meetings. Sure, on occasion people have spotted him repeating his affirmations and had a snigger at his expense. But he keeps repeating them and even repeated them for an interview when he was headhunted for an even bigger job. And now he is in one of the biggest jobs in British television. Who do you think has had the last laugh?

TAKE A PROBLEM-SOLVING APPROACH

Ever had a problem that feels like it won't go away? Perhaps you need to find a new client to stop your company from going bust. Maybe a nightmare boss is causing you daily grief. Or you have two weeks' worth of work to do – every week.

Sometimes positive thinking isn't enough. Yes, you can learn to manage the negative emotions caused by a problem. But sometimes you need to tackle the root cause of the problem. And knowing when to use each strategy is a part of becoming emotionally intelligent.

First check the nature of the problem – is it a tangible problem in the outside world or a problem in your inner world of how you are interpreting and reacting to it? For example, you might feel that your boss is criticizing you unfairly. But is your boss really being unfair? Or is it causing you anguish because you feel unreasonably unhappy about perfectly reasonable criticism? If it is the latter, then some of the emotion-based coping techniques that we have already discussed may be more useful in terms of challenging ANTs, putting things into perspective, and managing your physical sensations.

If, however, you identify that there is a tangible problem, then the following problem-solving steps may help you to tackle it:

1. *Define the problem.* The first step is to identify the root cause of the problem. You might feel stressed because you are being given too much work. But why are you being given too much work? Perhaps your boss is giving you more and more work to do because he trusts you more than others on the team. A short-term solution is to work long hours to get the work done. But the longer-term solution would be to talk to your boss. Or if you think that he is giving you more work because he is bullying you, you might need to think about getting HR involved.

2. *Generate possible solutions.* Take a few minutes to brainstorm at least a half-dozen or more ideas for tackling the problem. Remember that brainstorming is about being creative, so allow yourself the luxury of

coming up with outrageous ideas as well as practical ones. Having too few – perhaps only two or three – options limits your chances of picking the best one. On the other hand, brainstorming dozens and dozens of ideas provides diminishing returns.

3. *Create a shortlist.* The next step is to create a shortlist of the best options. Look through your brainstormed list and consider the practical impact of following each one through. Think about each idea – no matter how initially ridiculous it might seem. Sometimes the ridiculous ones can spark a more workable idea. For example, punching your boss might not be a good idea, but delivering a metaphorical punch with timely and incisive feedback could work. Eliminate unworkable ideas and combine ideas that seem to be similar until you have just three or four.

4. *Weigh up pros and cons.* Take your shortlist of options and write each one at the top of a separate sheet of paper. Draw a line down the middle of each sheet with the headings "pros" and "cons." List in the two columns all of the positive and negative consequences of taking each option.

5. *Make a choice.* Now evaluate the pros and cons associated with each of your options. Don't just total up the number of pros versus cons for each option. Sometimes a single pro can outweigh a dozen cons – or vice versa. Bear in mind that this is a qualitative process rather than quantitative. Unfortunately, very few choices in life are ever clear and even taking a

problem-solving approach is unlikely to "tell" you the answer. But which one now appeals to you the most? Follow through with your best option and accept that, in almost all cases, it is better to do something than do nothing.

I cannot underline strongly enough the power of writing down your thoughts when it comes to tackling a problem. Often, when our brains are wheeling with all of the options that are available to us, writing it down can allow our brains to analyze a problem in a different way. Simply seeing a list of options with pros and cons may help you to deduce the best route to take. Try it.

A final thought. A rational problem-solving approach can help you to identify useful ways to tackle some problems; however, it is not a tool that should be abused. Using it all of the time can lead to "analysis paralysis" – in which people become afraid to make any decisions without wanting to conduct a robust breakdown of the situation. Use it sparingly.

MAKE A LIST

Here's a quick tip to boost your motivation in just a few hours. Write all of the important tasks you need to accomplish over a number of hours. It could be one hour or ten, it doesn't matter.

But the trick is to write down an achievable list. Don't write every single task you need to complete. Especially when you are busy (and who isn't these days?), it will be too daunting. Just write down a few tasks that you should realistically be able to handle. If you have tasks that would take many hours to complete, then break them down into more manageable chunks. For example, if you need to organize a big meeting, then break it down into its component sections – ringing people to see if they have any items for the agenda, writing the agenda, emailing it to people, booking a room, and so on. And then put an achievable number of these chunks on your list.

Now get on with them. Complete them. And then cross them off your list.

You may not feel hugely impressed by your modest achievement, but it is still an achievement. And the brain is at once both remarkably complex and remarkably stupid. You can trick your own brain into thinking it has done a good job by setting yourself an achievable target and then achieving it. Your brain still feels good, releases a bucket load of feel-good chemicals into your blood, and helps you want to do more.

Now you can write a second list, but at this point adding a few further items. And each time you do it, you will gain momentum and find yourself becoming more and more motivated to tackle further items on your list.

I told you this was a quick one!

VISUALIZE SUCCESS

No one understands more than world-class athletes and sportspeople that success is a mental game. And that's why almost all of them employ visualization techniques to help them to excel.

The beauty of visualization is that it can foster a virtuous circle in the brain–body–behavior link. The neurobiology and psychopharmacology of it all is a book in itself. But the short version is that if you imagine yourself succeeding, then your brain sends nerve impulses to release chemicals that promote positive emotions. Say goodbye to nervousness and tension. Say hello to confidence and enthusiasm.

Visualization is not a quick fix, though. Topflight athletes spend months and months visualizing success. Even for sports such as javelin throwing or running the 100 meters that laypeople like you and I might think were rather straightforward, competitors routinely spend months picturing what it would look and feel like.

When you are preparing to face a tough event – a presentation, an interview, an appraisal, a confrontation – practice visualizing how you would like it to go. It doesn't matter if you don't know exactly what the room looks like. It doesn't even matter if you have never met the people and don't know what they look like.

It is more important to run through the sequence of events in your mind. Let's take an example of going to meet a particularly important client. Imagine yourself wearing your favorite suit, smiling and offering a firm handshake to the client. Picture yourselves sitting down. Rehearse what you plan to say and the kind of body language that you hope to project. Anticipate the kinds of questions and objections that the client might raise and the responses that you would give. Picture the conversation going smoothly with the client nodding and agreeing with your proposals. Envisage the meeting finishing with another firm handshake as the delighted client escorts you from the room.

Do it in a quiet place so that you don't have phone calls or email pings interrupting your mental movie. Add as much detail to the picture as you can. Spend as long as possible on each visualization, and do it frequently.

Despite the fact that you don't move a muscle, visualization should be hard work. If you do it in a half-hearted way, you will get half-hearted results. If you take the time and make the effort to imagine a scenario in greater clarity, the results can be surprising.

All that remains is for you to try it.

USE EMOTIONAL ANCHORS

I have a confession to make. *Pretty Woman* is one of my all-time favorite movies. It makes me smile. It was on television the other night and I watched it (again – for about the hundredth time). I just grin for the duration of the film.

We all have triggers – events, songs, smells, tastes, possessions, and even memories – that make us feel a certain way. Why do you think so many executives have photographs of their family on their desks? Because they know that even the simple act of looking at photographs of loved ones can raise our spirits.

Emotional anchors are often naff and a bit embarrassing to the outside world. They have a powerful effect on us because of their particular relevance and importance to us – perhaps they remind us of a happy place or time. But to others, our emotional anchors can seem stupid or clichéd. It really doesn't matter what your emotional anchors are.

What is important is that our emotions can be consciously manipulated by the anchors we keep around us.

I used to share my office with a colleague who kept his son's baby teeth in a little jar in his desk. He would get the jar out and rattle them when he was feeling troubled. I know an executive who has an aspidistra on his desk that he grew from a cutting that he took from his own garden. He cleans the big waxy leaves when he feels the weight of work getting him down and it relaxes him.

Tell me that you don't smile and laugh when you leaf through old photos. I just wouldn't believe you if you said that you didn't.

Another of my personal anchors is a Molton Brown room fragrance called "Air of Joy." When I first started traveling for business, I noticed that a lot of swanky hotels stocked Molton Brown products. I came to believe that if I could one day afford to buy the fragrance, then I would have "made it" in my career. In actuality, it costs no more than a bottle of house wine in a restaurant. But a couple of squirts when I'm feeling lethargic or dejected reminds me that I have "made it," lifting my mood.

I did warn you that emotional anchors could seem naff!

But emotional anchors can be both negative and positive. They can evoke bad feelings as well as good. An unhappy song can remind us of a painful time in our lives. A notepad with scribblings you took in a particularly stressful meeting can make you relive that stress all over again. So make sure that you surround your workplace with positive emotional anchors. Put any negative ones in the bin.

So what would your (positive) emotional anchors be?

WALK TALL

Do you ever imagine that your body is being controlled by a giant invisible puppet master? No? Well, maybe you should.

This tip is about your posture and body language. And, surprise surprise, it is important because of that brain–body–behavior link.

We all know that in interviews we should never sit with our legs crossed or our arms folded because interviewers might take it as a sign of nervousness. But it turns out that good body language is doubly important – not just because it can project a certain impression but also because it can foster positive emotions in ourselves too.

Want to be more confident? Then act as if you are confident.

Walk into a room as if you own it. Imagine a piece of string attached to the top of your head. Now imagine that a giant invisible puppet master is lifting the piece of string, pulling your head up. Try it now – whether you are standing on a train platform or slumped in a comfortable chair as you read this. Imagine that someone is pulling your body upwards. The first thing that would happen is that you would straighten your back. And then the muscles in your neck would lengthen. In fact, all the muscles in your body would elongate as you reach your full height.

As simple an act as holding yourself upright will affect that brain–body–behavior link to push negative emotions out of your mind.

When you are in meetings, imagine that a giant invisible puppet master is controlling your arms. What do confident people do? Think about films you have seen with corporate hot shots waving their arms around to illustrate points. They punch the air; they smack their fists into their palms. They point and make big, expansive gestures. They use their hands and arms to underline their arguments. Your elbows are not surgically attached to your rib cage. So free your arms.

If you behave as if you are a bigwig, then you will start to believe that you are one too.

HANDLE SETBACKS

We all experience setbacks in our lives. Maybe it is the failure to get a promotion or win a major client. Perhaps it is the disappointment of having your business plan turned down or being made redundant. But a big part of self-direction is understanding how setbacks affect you and how to motivate yourself to overcome them. Again, the difference between a successful person and a failure often comes down to the ability to get up again after being knocked down.

Psychologists have spent decades researching the stages that we go through when we experience major setbacks in life. Understanding these stages gives us the chance to move through the five stages to recovery more quickly:

1. *Denial.* We're in shock. We feel numb. Our first reaction is that we refuse to believe what has happened. "I can't believe they turned me down." "I can't believe

this is really happening to me." We don't know how to behave, as we cannot quite come to terms with what has happened.

2. *Anger*. After denying it, we often get angry. We feel victimized. "Why me?" "This is so unfair!" "The bastards!" We may complain or blame others for our loss. We can take it out on friends and colleagues by lashing out or pushing them away without good reason. Sometimes we internalize the anger and become infuriated with ourselves.

3. *Disorientation and depression*. Next, we often feel confused and unhappy. "What did I do wrong?" "I feel so tired – I want to be on my own." "This is hopeless – I can't go on any more." We feel physically and emotionally exhausted. A sense of despair consumes us and we can't seem to do anything. We may find it difficult to sleep because automatic negative thoughts are running through our heads. This is the most difficult stage to deal with.

4. *Acceptance*. Eventually – and for some people it can take weeks or months while others might need only hours or days – we come to terms with the setback. We recognize that our situation has changed. We feel less emotional about the setback and realize that life must go on.

5. *Renewal*. Finally, we are able to resume work and life as normal. We may still think about the setback, but for the most part we are able to think about it in a more rational way, rather than being drowned by the

emotions that it evoked at first. We are able to make plans and think about the future again.

While these are the general stages of dealing with setbacks, we do not always experience them in the same way. Sometimes we experience one stage for days and another for mere minutes. We might experience only the briefest moment of denial before becoming incensed by bad news. Or one setback might cause us to feel angry while another makes us feel incredibly depressed. The pattern is rarely the same for different incidents or for different people. However, understanding these stages gives you a chance to identify which stage you are in and then accelerate the pace with which you move through them to renewal.

DEVELOP YOUR EMOTIONAL RESILIENCE

The thing about setbacks is that they are all, literally, only in your mind. Consider that two people both get turned down for a promotion. While one person may suffer weeks of disorientation and depression, another might decide the next day to take steps to work towards the next opportunity for promotion. Few setbacks are physical – yes you may suffer a tangible loss of income, but people at work generally do not inflict bodily injury on each other. So whether you recover quickly or not is up to how you perceive the setback and become resilient to it.

Here are some steps to take to recover from the stages of setbacks more quickly:

1. *Denial.* One trick to move through denial more quickly is called "constructive acknowledgement." Rather than denying the problem, you acknowledge the reality of what is happening to you – but in a positive way that will help you to move on. Write down the negative thoughts you are having and then look for positive ways in which you can overcome them. For example, if you have been fired, you might write down, "I will have to update my CV and apply for jobs now." If you have failed to hit a major project milestone, you could decide, "I need to call the team together for an emergency meeting first thing in the morning to discuss next steps." By acknowledging a disappointment and thinking about actions to take, you will help yourself to avoid denying the problem for too long.

2. *Anger.* Becoming emotionally intelligent, you should now realize that dealing with negative emotions is important. There are two main ways in which to release the negative emotions. The first is to use the tips we have already discussed – in terms of monitoring and managing your physical sensations and symptoms, and challenging automatic negative thoughts to dissipate the anger. Others find that it helps to channel the anger. Find a soundproof room to scream and swear and yell and punch soft furnishings until your throat feels hoarse and you are too tired to feel angry.

3. *Disorientation and depression.* You will need all of your emotional skills to fend off feelings of despair and apathy. This is the most challenging stage for most people to overcome. While you may feel like being on your own, you need to force yourself to be with other people. Talking to colleagues or friends about your feelings will dampen down your unhappiness, but it is a step that many people – especially men – find difficult. But you must realize that while you may make yourself temporarily vulnerable by talking about your feelings, you will be able to recover from them that much more quickly. When you do find yourself on your own, your mind will make you want to blame yourself. So it is up to you to identify and challenge automatic negative thoughts. Write down your ANTs and counter each of them with a positive statement about yourself.

4. *Acceptance.* When you have managed to overcome your feelings of unhappiness, you need to take more constructive action. Remember when you were in denial, you made some notes on short-term actions to deal with the setback. Now is the time to follow through with action. Refer back to your personal vision and SMART goals and think about further medium- and longerterm actions that you can take to get yourself back on track. It will be only a matter of time before you find yourself moving through to ...

5. *Renewal.* Congratulations – you've made it.

04

Interpersonal Savvy

Interpersonal savvy, or the skills of being able to understand, influence, persuade, win over, and motivate other people, is the pinnacle of emotional intelligence. There are some rules that apply to everyone – for instance almost everyone responds to good listening skills and efforts to build rapport. And helping others to deal with their emotions will win you many friends for life too. Imagine how people will warm to you if you can lift their spirits when they are sad, calm them down when they are angry, or alleviate their fears when they are troubled.

But becoming a true expert in emotional intelligence means that you need to identify the right technique for influencing each particular individual in every different situation. No two people are quite the same – they each have their different motivators, triggers, and personality characteristics. Some people respond to challenges. Few people respond well to threats. Others might respond to encouragement and flattery. Still others may need your understanding and sympathy to persuade them to take action. And it is up to you, the emotionally intelligent individual, to figure out how best to handle different people in the many situations you will come across.

Interpersonal savvy can be broken down into four key skills that will help you to achieve your goals in work and life:

- Empathy and rapport – building a vital precursor to interpersonal effectiveness.
- Communication – asking people for what you want or need from them.
- Building rewarding relationships – building long-term and mutually useful relationships.
- Tackling unsatisfactory relationships – dealing with relationships when they go wrong.

At the end of the day, interpersonal savvy is basically the science of making other people do what you want them to do. You won't often see it written down in such plain terms – because we live in a politically correct world that frowns upon such directness. We are supposed to work for mutual benefit and toward organizational goals. Well, let's dispense with that nonsense shall we? Use the skills of interpersonal savvy to further your own personal goals.

EMPATHY AND RAPPORT

Just as the foundation for managing your own emotions effectively is to become more aware of them, the foundation for influencing others effectively is to become more aware of what they think and feel by empathizing with them.

How would you react if a stranger were to blunder into

your office and ask you to do a piece of work for them? Understandably, you might be a bit peeved. So never try to talk business or ask a favor of anyone that you have only just met. Whether they are a VIP from a prospective client company or a colleague in another department, the rule is the same. Rapport is an essential part of doing business. Unless you are reading a translation of this book in Japan, this rule applies to you.

Think about it. In job interviews, the most likeable candidate often wins out over the more skilled and experienced (but less warm and friendly) candidate. When a company is choosing a new advertising agency to work with, they might say that they picked the one with the most original ideas – but often they plump for the one that they felt most comfortable with. Even when people are asked for favors in your office, who do you think they are most likely to help out first? The person with the more urgent request or the person that they like more?

Empathy and rapport build liking. And the more difficult or demanding your request, the more you need the other person to like you.

The key to creating empathy and rapport is listening. Most people are guilty of talking too much and listening too little. Or they hear the words but don't listen to the meaning. But only by listening and taking steps to demonstrate that we are listening can we build the rapport that is the precursor to exercising influence and persuasion over others.

The skill of building empathy and rapport can be broken down into a number of steps:

- listening;
- reading emotional cues;
- asking questions;
- demonstrating listening and sensitivity.
- making eye contact.

Listen, listen, listen

Let's face it. A lot of the people we encounter are really quite boring. How often had you had to feign interest in someone's hernia operation, goatherding holiday, color scheme for their new home, or argument with their spouse?

But the danger of not paying attention is that you might not catch the one or two key sentences that will allow you to understand what makes them tick. And it is only when you understand what makes them tick that you can successfully maneuver them into doing what you want them to do.

Too often, we rush to finish other people's sentences or try to offer advice or judgment while they are talking. But if you want to influence them, show that you are willing to be influenced first. Listen.

Probably the best single technique for improving your listening skills is to summarize and paraphrase. Wait until a natural pause arises in the conversation and then restate in just one or two sentences what they have been saying. Think along the lines of: "So you seem to be saying ...," "If I understand correctly then ...," and "Let me get this straight...."

I'll give you three reasons why it is so powerful.

1. *Many people do not express themselves particularly clearly.*
   What they want to say may not be what they end up
   saying. Especially when they are emotional, they may
   garble their words and mix their messages. So putting
   into your own words what you think they said and
   repeating it back to them allows you to check that you
   understood them correctly.
2. *Summarizing and paraphrasing shows that you are
   listening.* It gives the speaker ongoing feedback and
   encouragement to keep talking. And the more they talk,
   the more you will learn about what makes them tick.
3. *It helps to embed further into your consciousness what
   they are saying.* I am probably not the only person who
   has ever been guilty of hearing words but not listening
   to the meaning.

You are a bright person. I know that you know how to
listen. But the question is whether you do it as often as you
should.

Read emotional cues

Would it surprise you if I told you that you were leaking at
this very moment?

No, I don't mean like that. What I'm trying to explain is
that your body language is constantly communicating even
when you think you have nothing to say. We leak non-verbal
messages all of the time through our facial expressions and
body language. In fact, our words make up only a small
percentage of our impact on other people – 7 percent of the

impact to be precise. The other 93 percent of our impact is made by our body language and tone of voice.

We'll come to how you can make use of your body language later. For now though, pay attention to the non-verbal cues of the people that you are listening to. The message that comes out of their mouths is sometimes less interesting than the one that their body language is telling you.

Most people find it difficult to talk about their emotions. Especially at work, people believe that expressing emotion is tantamount to showing weakness. But getting people to show you their emotions is a powerful tool for winning them over. Offer a shoulder to cry on, and you have a friend and ally for life.

If you are looking out for body language cues, they are usually easy to spot. For example, when someone claims, "I'm fine, really. I'm not bothered by it," but their voice is shaky and tears are welling up in their eyes, you know that they really are not fine and they are very much bothered by something.

In many situations, people do not deny certain feelings outright. But they may share only part of the story. "I can't believe that bitch got the job" presents itself as frustration by a colleague that she got the job. But a bit of probing on your part might expose the fact that the speaker is really upset at the senior managers, and not really the colleague, for not having recognized his or her talents.

A full list of cues is too long to list extensively – and I'm sure you know what to look for. But an abbreviated checklist includes:

- Hands and feet – twitching and tapping, wringing of hands or jiggling of feet.
- Posture – hunched/slumped versus upright.
- Facial expressions – everything from frowns and lip chewing through to unconvincing smiles and avoiding eye contact. Look out for blushing, flushing, or pallor when people are scared as well.
- Voice quality – how does volume/pitch/ pace compare with the person's normal speaking voice? And is there hesitation as he or she speaks?
- Breathing – is it faster or slower than normal? Any deep intakes or sudden breaths out?

A warning though. Sometimes there really may be no hidden messages. If, for example, someone says, "I have so many problems right now," it could mean that they want to talk about their feelings. But it could equally mean that they have more work than they are happy with. They may be looking to vent momentary frustration rather than enter into a discussion about their feelings. So don't look for deeper meanings when there may be none.

Ask questions

Conversations are like the tips of icebergs. People usually only offer a part of the whole story. Buried below the surface lies the truth, the background, and everything you need to understand before you wade in with your opinions.

You can't really go wrong with a question. Questions demonstrate that you are interested and paying attention.

Even seemingly throwaway questions such as "Nice suit – when did you get it?" or "Where did you get those lovely earrings?" are almost certain to win you brownie points with just about everybody.

In trying to understand people, a closed question – one that can be answered by a single "Yes" or "No" – is a waste of a question. Questions should open further avenues for discussion rather than close them off. In fact, closed questions such as, "So will you be able to make that meeting?" and "You're happy to do that report by Wednesday, right?" can be subtle signals that you are keen to end a conversation.

Open questions are the key to unlocking a wealth of information and begin with "what," "why," and "when," as well as "how" and "where." But you knew that already. More usefully, consider using the STAR method to ensure that you gather all of the information that you might need to understand properly what you are being told:

- Situation – "What happened?" "When did this happen?" "Who was involved?"
- Task – "What was your/their intention?" "What were you/they trying to do?" And "Why?"
- Action – "What did you/they actually do?" "What did they/you do in response to that?" "What happened next?" (And repeat "What happened next?" as required until the speaker has exhausted the actions taken by the various parties.)
- Result – "What was the outcome?" Or "When will you find out what is going to happen next?" "How do you feel?"

The questions are designed to prompt you rather than be used verbatim, so don't simply fire them all at someone. While it is important to gather as much information as possible, asking too many questions will make a discussion seem more like an interrogation than a conversation.

Look out for any mismatches between the speaker's words and body language too. If the speaker is leaking non-verbal cues indicating that he or she isn't voluntarily telling you the whole truth, comment on it – "I can't help noticing that you seem ..." – then let that person respond to your observation. More often than not, it will open up yet more avenues for discussion, as the speaker will take it as an opportunity to vent their true feelings.

Demonstrate listening and sensitivity

Here's a question for you. Would you rather people thought of you as understanding and supportive, or arrogant and condescending? Amazingly, the latter is exactly how most people choose to portray themselves by offering advice too early.

Jump in too soon with advice and you are implicitly saying: "Your problem is all very well. But with my superior intellect and greater experience, here is how I think you should deal with your situation."

Yes, you may actually be brighter and more experienced. But no one likes a show-off, do they? So shut up for now, curb your inclination to advise, and learn instead to demonstrate your listening skills and empathy.

Good listeners do more than merely listen. They actively demonstrate that they are listening through a dance of verbal and non-verbal cues. If you have ever had a conversation with someone who didn't nod, didn't smile, didn't react to what you said in any way, you will know why these cues are necessary.

Excellent listeners use a combination of three dynamic cues to show that they are listening:

- Nodding – to signal agreement with what is being said. It shows that you are following the gist of the conversation. On the other hand, shakes of the head are useful when a speaker is telling you about a difficult state of affairs or an unpleasant emotion.
- Flashing – using facial expressions to match the mood and expressions of a speaker. For example, you frown to show that you appreciate how heartbreaking a situation must have been, or smile to parallel a positive experience.
- Murmuring – words and phrases such as "Go on," "I see," and "Yes," or small noises such as "Mmm" or "Uh-huh" encourage the other person to keep talking.

But the next stage on from demonstrating that you are listening is to convey the fact that you empathize with the speaker – that you not only understand but also appreciate the emotions they are experiencing.

The key to empathizing is to imagine yourself in their situation. This is where your enhanced awareness of your own emotions comes into play: How would you feel in the particular situation? This is still not the time to give advice yet, so focus only on how you would feel – not what you would have done differently. Share your appreciation of how the person feels and validate their emotions with phrases such as:

- "I'd have been terrified too."
- "I would have felt that way as well."
- "I can't believe he took his anger out on you like that!"
- "That's awful."

Empathy is hard work – especially when you have never had any experience of the situation that is being described to you. For instance if someone is telling you about the loss of a loved one or the progression of a horrible disease, you might sometimes only be able to say: "I can't even begin to imagine how that feels."

But every now and then empathy can be difficult because someone may describe a problem or situation that sounds petty or inconsequential to us. For example, I have observed two colleagues shouting and swearing at each other over a borrowed stapler! In such situations, there are two options for coping. If you are looking to build mutually beneficial relationships, then don't fake empathy. Instead, use bland statements that imply that you understand: "I've never been in that situation myself, but I'm sorry to hear that you had such a terrible time of it." On the other hand, if you are looking to build a relationship in order to influence that person and ultimately get him or her to do what you want, then fake it. Pretend. Even if you couldn't care less, say that you do and make sure that your face and rest of your body language don't leak the truth. As Harry S. Truman once said: "Always be sincere, even if you don't mean it."

The power of empathy cannot be overestimated. Because corporate cultures usually frown upon the display of emotion, your use of empathy can make people feel really good about themselves – to know that it is OK to show their emotion. Showing that you appreciate their situation and are sensitive to it is a sure-fire way to build rapport. Do it regularly and you will have them eating out of the palm of your hand.

Make eye contact, don't stare

Ever told a lie? To cover up a little untruth, you probably made an effort to appear nonchalant and to maintain eye contact. And that's how most people give themselves away – by making too much eye contact in an attempt to avoid appearing shifty.

We all know how important it is to hold someone's gaze when we are having a conversation. But it turns out it is slightly more complicated than just looking all of the time. Eye contact is one of the most powerful non-verbal cues we have for building rapport. And there is a fundamental rule that governs how to use it effectively: When someone else is speaking, you look at them; when you speak, you can look away.

Let's examine that in a bit more depth.

When someone else is speaking, you need to look at them pretty much all of the time. You can't achieve 100 percent of the time – for a start you need to blink. And if, for instance, they make gestures with their hands or point at something, then you need to follow their gaze. So somewhere in the region of 80 percent to 90 percent of the time is more realistic.

When it is your turn to speak, however, you should look at the person you are speaking to only 50 per cent of the time. Looking at them too much could easily make them think that you are a slightly unhinged character. In fact, if you ever want to make someone feel uncomfortable – perhaps without them realizing exactly why they don't feel at ease – then staring into their eyes unrelentingly will do it.

Watch carefully the next time you engage a person in conversation. Encounters in a shop or with other customer service staff don't count, as most of the time they are too bored with their jobs to bother with decent eye contact. The next time you see a friend, colleague, or acquaintance, watch their eyes as they tell you about their day or relate an anecdote about themselves. More often than not, they will break eye contact for a significant proportion of the time they are talking, as if they are seeing the scene that they are describing to you.

The converse is also true. If you ever need to signal boredom – to get rid of someone, for example, who is perched on the end of your desk telling you an anecdote about his or her tedious social life when you have urgent work to do – simply drop your eye contact down to 10 or 20 percent. Keep listening but look at your computer screen or pick up a pen and start to make notes for that urgent report you need to complete. The person should get the message.

So there you go: eye contact, not staring.

COMMUNICATION

Communication is an exchange of thoughts and ideas. But the key word here is "exchange." Despite the power that comes from asking questions and listening, there comes a time when you will need to do some of the talking too. Long-term relationships are about exchange and reciprocity – discovering each other's wants and needs, asking for help from each other, and finding ways to respond to each other's requests. Doing all the asking and no telling works for a short while. Certainly, asking lots of questions of people is a great way to captivate strangers for an evening at a party. But it isn't much use in building long-term relationships.

To be effective at work, we need to tell people what we want from them. We need to be able to share our thoughts and opinions and make requests of them. We need to stand up for our rights – but treading the fine line between aggression and passivity – by asserting ourselves. If we are unhappy, we might need to give people feedback and constructive criticism about their behavior.

Whatever your goals in life, communication is critical. But you already knew that – it's hardly a new message. The next handful of techniques illustrates how to fuse words and emotion toproduce irresistible communication.

Reinforce rapport through self-disclosure

I used to work with someone who was perfect. David had a first-class degree from a top university and an MBA from a top business school. He produced work that was always on time and delighted clients. He spoke three languages and was an accomplished cook. Oh, he had a lovely girlfriend too. How the rest of us hated him.

People are suspicious of perfection. Would you feel comfortable confessing how you had single-handedly managed to crash the company's computer system to someone who had never made a mistake in his or her life? Would you be happy to admit your failings to someone who had none?

So here's the point. If you do not reveal a few of your own failings and failures to other people, other people will probably avoid you altogether. But it could get worse than mere avoidance. We used to joke that David was a secret deviant in the bedroom. No one could be that perfect. Just as nature abhors a vacuum, human nature looks to fill the void with gossip and speculation. People start to wonder: Why don't I know anything about this mysterious person? What are they hiding? If you don't tell them anything about yourself, they will make stuff up.

A good way to ease yourself into disclosing is to share anecdotes about mistakes you have made and lessons you have learnt. Use the acronym TALE to compose good learning anecdotes:

- **T**ask – what was the task that you were trying to do?
- **A**ction – what actions did you take to achieve the task?
- **L**earning – what happened? And what did you learn from the problems you encountered or the mistakes that you made?
- **E**valuation – evaluate whether you are sure that this is a story that you want to share. Who would be the right audience for it – your boss, your peers, or more junior

people? What tone should you adopt to get your point across – serious or self-deprecating? Does the anecdote show you off in a good light or make you sound preachy and arrogant?

Disclosing minor failings and failures shows that you are human too. You make mistakes; you have weaknesses. Showing your vulnerable side to others allows or even encourages them to share with you. But be careful not to overdo it.

I used to work with a colleague who used to share just a little too much. If Helen wasn't splitting up from her boyfriend for the fifth or sixth time, she was having problems with her landlord. There was also the health scare when she had to go to hospital for a scan. And that was way before she even started on the endless problems she was having with work.

TMI – too much information!

Remember that disclosing is about allowing a trickle of information out about you. It is not about opening the floodgates on every tragedy that has ever happened to you. End of lecture.

Express your emotions

Just as people feel uncomfortable relating their failings to others who appear to have none, they are reluctant to express their emotions to others who refuse to do the same.

People often feel that the workplace is not the place for emotions. But no matter how much we may be discouraged from talking about them, we still experience them and suffer the impact of others' emotions. Whether we want to or not, we "leak" emotions – showing our annoyance, anger, unhappiness, or fear – through our behavior, body language, and tone of voice all of the time. So why not clear the air by talking about them? Learning to talk about your emotions encourages others to do the same. In turn, understanding their emotions will enable you to influence them more effectively.

However, given that emotions are taboo in many workplaces, always express your emotions on a one-to-one basis. People seem to find emotion all the more uncomfortable when it is displayed in public.

Expressing your emotions is also a clever tool to lead into discussing difficult situations and how to resolve them. Let's say that you feel overburdened by a huge workload and want help from your manager. Perhaps a customer is taking his frustration out on you. Or the team is suffering from low morale. Talking about your feelings allows you to broach the topic of how to tackle problems – getting help for yourself, facing up to the customer, or discussing ways to boost team morale.

This is another opportunity to build upon your foundation of emotional intelligence skills. Having worked on your self-awareness of your own emotions should allow you to share what you are feeling with others in an appropriate fashion. Some tips:

- *Audit all of the feelings that you are experiencing.* This will help you to sort through the feelings that you want to convey. For example, if you feel stressed by long hours at work, you might be feeling a multitude of feelings: "I'm unhappy that I'm not producing good quality work," "I'm depressed because I'm not getting to see my family," "I feel angry that my boss hasn't appreciated my hard work," and "I feel embarrassed that I am having to ask for help."

- *Identify what you want to convey.* Rather than blurting out all of your feelings, your emotional intelligence should allow you to work out which emotions it would be useful to share. For example, "I'm unhappy that I'm not producing good quality work" and "I feel embarrassed that I am having to ask for help" will probably elicit a more sympathetic and productive response from your manager than "I feel angry that you aren't appreciating my hard work."

- *Choose the right way to phrase your feelings.* For example, "depressed" is a very evocative word and some unsympathetic people (of which there are, unfortunately, quite a few at work) could take it as too great a human failing to show at work. Perhaps "unhappy" or "down" might be more appropriate in some settings. Another issue is to consider the extent of your relationship with the other person – for example are you expressing your emotions to a colleague who is also a close friend or your boss with whom you only have a working relationship? You need to judge your organization's culture and the emotional intelligence of the person to whom you are preparing to disclose. What kind of terminology would they appreciate?

Again, be careful not to share too much. Just as people feel uncomfortable with people who appear to be emotionless robots, there is such a thing as too much emotion as well. Breaking down and confessing the extent of your unhappiness on a weekly basis would probably damage your reputation and future prospects.

It's impossible to define "too much" or even "not enough," as it depends entirely on the culture of your organization or team. For example, I used to work in one company where the senior managers were fixated on the idea of giving and receiving feedback. Almost the moment we left a client, someone would ask: "How was I in that meeting?" They always wanted to know how others felt, and were keen to share their own emotions. Despite it being a company with fewer than 30 people, it wasn't uncommon to have a colleague crying in the office on an almost weekly basis. But then the next organization that I worked for seemed to stifle emotions. No one wanted to hear about how you felt – they just wanted to get on with the work at hand. They believed very much that work was for work, and home was for emotion.

Tread carefully.

Disclose secrets with care

When is a secret not a secret? Answer – when it is shared.

Disclosing anecdotes about mistakes you have made is a good way to build rapport. Expressing your emotions also deepens relationships. But be careful not to disclose secrets such as a job offer that you are thinking about or major indiscretions and wrongdoings.

A secret almost always gets out – even if you whisper it to someone, ask them not to share it and explain why. Sometimes it is because people like to talk. Even if they feel uncomfortable sharing their own mistakes or emotions, they are often more than happy to share other people's misdeeds and faux pas. Sometimes they do it because they want to show off to others that they are privy to information that others don't know. Sometimes what they define as a secret may differ from your definition, or they blurt it out without meaning to. Or maybe they think that telling their best friend or spouse might not count as breaking a confidence.

For so many reasons, be careful with secrets.

As a very rough rule of thumb, there's a formula for predicting the number of people who actually know your secret, based on the number that you think know about it:

> ❗ $R = N^2 + 1$ (where R = the real number of people who actually know your
> ⬤ secret; and N = the number of people you think know your secret)

So if you have told just one person your secret ($N = 1$), then $R = 1^2 + 1 = 2$ – two people probably know your secret. If you have told three people ($N = 3$), then $R = 3^2 + 1 = 10$. In other words, 10 people probably know your secret. Not so secret any more, is it?

But it's worth mentioning secrets for another reason. If you share your emotions and minor mistakes to others, they will share theirs with you. And that is where the sharing should stop. A relationship is a bond between two individuals

– not a relationship between two individuals and their best friends or closest colleagues or partners at home.

Admit it, you like to hear a bit of news or gossip. But while it is perfectly acceptable to listen to rumors or gossip, you must always keep confidences. Otherwise, how do you think someone would react if they ever found out that you had broken a confidence?

Make effective requests

A big part of communication is making effective requests of other people. But there is a trick to it.

In my early twenties, I was once on holiday with friends. We stayed at a hotel with a swimming pool that was usually busy, but one evening we found it empty. There was a small sign saying, "Please do not swim until 6 pm." But we only had 20 minutes to wait so decided to jump into the pool anyway. Minutes later, a lifeguard came out and explained that he had only an hour ago emptied two canisters of chlorine into the pool to sterilize it and that undiluted chlorine can cause skin blistering. Clambering out of the pool, boy did we feel stupid.

The sign had told us what to do – but it hadn't explained why.

When people are told to do anything, they often do precisely the opposite because they resent being lectured to, or they think they have a better idea. In making requests and issuing instructions, it is not enough merely to tell them what to do – you also need to explain why.

It may sound obvious, but so many people don't explain

the reasons behind a request. Especially when we get busy, we may forget. Or we assume that the reason should be obvious. But as an emotionally intelligent individual, you need to remember that we all perceive reality in different ways. What is completely obvious to you may not occur to other people. You need to empathize and think about how they may feel as a result of your request or instruction, and prepare to respond to those emotions.

So this is a simple one: Don't tell; explain.

But as with most rules, don't overdo it. You should explain why you are asking a colleague to attend a meeting instead of you. But of course explaining in great detail and asking your colleague's feelings when you only want to ask him or her to lend you a pen would be silly.

Finally, make sure that you thank people after they have followed through with your requests. Now, you may think that I shouldn't need to stress the importance of thanking people, but surveys repeatedly show that people feel that they don't get enough gratitude at work – so I apologize if you are already in the top 10 percent of the workforce who does express their gratitude enough. And if you are like the rest of us, just make sure you thank people for helping you out.

Give constructive feedback

Hey it happens. No matter how effective your request or instruction, other people will sometimes let you down or fail to deliver.

Feedback is an essential tool for helping people to understand the consequences of their actions. When those consequences are quantifiable – for instance a delivery was late or a report was full of mistakes – it is far easier to give feedback. The situation is more likely to provide a right and a wrong, allowing you to cite clear fact-based evidence to back up your criticisms.

But often the consequences are a matter of perception – you felt that your boss was unfair to you or that a colleague was too pushy with a client. They probably felt the precise opposite. The consequences are open to interpretation, which makes the feedback trickier to give.

In either case, no one likes to be criticized. Accordingly, incorporating your understanding of emotions into providing constructive feedback will make it a far less painful process.

Some guidelines:

- *Think about the feelings that your feedback is likely to elicit.* Consider the magnitude of the incident or error and what you already know about their personality and willingness to express emotions. Might they become defensive and deny the issue? Or are they more likely to be surprised and upset by it?
- *Ask permission to give them feedback.* Rather than blurting out a harsh criticism, ask if you can talk to them about the situation or piece of work. It allows them to choose a more appropriate time and place to discuss it if they are busy.
- *Be timely with your feedback.* Feedback is most effective when details of the incident are still fresh in everyone's minds. It is unfortunately all too common

for managers or colleagues to wait weeks or months until an annual appraisal to "stick the knife in" with feedback, by which time the details of the incident are too hazy for the individual to be able to learn anything from it.

- *Make it clear that you are discussing your interpretation of an incident.* Say "I," not "you." "I think" and "I feel" make it clear that these are your beliefs and feelings, whereas "you" statements can sound accusatory. You cannot know their intentions, so don't say, "You always put the rest of the team's needs ahead of mine," when you can only legitimately say, "I feel that you put the rest of the team's needs ahead of mine." As another example, you cannot know how someone felt, so don't say, "You were angry and unfair," if you mean, "I felt hurt because I felt that you were being angry and unfair."

- *Cite evidence to support the feedback.* If there are facts, then use them: "The client phoned me the other day to complain that the parcel was damaged." But when the situation involves feelings, refer to the observations that you made. So rather than "You looked bored in that client meeting," explain, "I thought you were bored because I noticed that you were much quieter than usual and you were doodling in your notepad."

- *Give the other person an opportunity to respond.* By citing evidence and making it clear that you are discussing your reading of the incident, you are allowing them to refute your interpretation and explain their actual intentions. "That's what I saw, but how do you feel about that?"

- *Validate their emotions.* Listen to what they are saying and pay attention to the messages their body language is sending you. If they seem upset, then do say, "I'm sorry if I have upset you." Never apologize for providing feedback, but do apologize for causing negative emotions.

Feedback is not just pointing out errors. So the last step is to work together to consider what actions might need to be taken, for example if a mistake needs correcting or ground rules for future behavior need to be established. Ask what the recipient of feedback thinks they should do next. If they struggle to answer, make sure you have a helpful suggestion.

Assert yourself

Evolution has a lot to answer for. The "fight or flight" response has been programmed into us for thousands of years and hundreds of generations. When challenged, our ancestors either beat an adversary to death (fight) or ran away (flight). They didn't try to negotiate with saber-toothed tigers or spear-wielding rivals. So it's hardly surprising that in the modern workplace we find it easier to slip into old habits of being too aggressive (fight) or too passive (flight), rather than finding some third way through sticky situations.

When other people make requests of us that do not meet our wants or needs, we should stand up for our rights. But it is a prized skill to be able to tread that fine line between aggression and passivity, to be assertive all of the time.

You know the feeling. A colleague asks you to do a favor that you really don't want to do – but you swallow your objections and do it anyway. Or you manage to decline the request but end up showing your irritation or even anger.

Remember that communication is made up not only of the words you use, but also of your body language and tone of voice. Here are some tips for asserting yourself effectively:

- *Listen to the other person's request fully.* Use dynamic listening cues to show that you are listening. No matter how much you want to disagree or interrupt, let the speaker finish their request. If you interrupt too early, you might miss a critical piece of information and end up looking terribly foolish.

- *Acknowledge the other person's position.* Paraphrase and summarize briefly to show that you have understood the request. "I understand that you need someone to come into work this weekend or else the project won't get completed."

- *Explain why you are declining the request.* You need to provide compelling reasons for not being able to respond to their request. Keep your vision and personal goals in mind. If you have decided to prioritize outside interests ahead of your career, then make a stand. Explain that you had promised to take your children to the zoo this weekend.

- *Acknowledge the request again and repeat your reasons.* Often the danger of becoming aggressive or passive is greatest when the other person keeps reiterating their request. Your tactic each time should be to acknowledge the request and repeat your reasons. This is sometimes called the broken record technique – repeating your acknowledgement and reasons again and again and again. For example, "Yes, but I need to take my children to the zoo this weekend," "Yes, I realize it's a big problem, but I made this promise that I really can't break," "Yes, but I've broken too many family promises to break this one too."

- *Pay attention to rising physical sensations and symptoms that might steer you towards being aggressive or passive.* Relax those shoulders, control your breathing, and keep a neutral expression on your face.
- *Keep control of your voice.* Watch your volume and pace. Allowing your voice to rise in volume or speed up could be an initial sign of aggression. Speaking more quietly or hesitatingly could mean that you are slipping into passivity.

Another tactic that may help you to be assertive rather than aggressive or passive is to ask for a time out when people make requests that you would like to decline. "I understand what you're saying, but can I think about it for a few minutes?" It doesn't work all of the time, as you may need to make a decision there and then. But on the occasions that you can, creating a time out for yourself will allow you to marshal your thoughts and prepare your argument for declining the request assertively.

Learn to say no, but ...

Ever felt in an argument that you were butting your head against a wall? No matter how assertive you might be in stating your case, your boss/colleague/ customer is not willing to take "No" for an answer. If you are faced with an emotionally unintelligent person, they could easily get angry and turn the discussion into a blazing row.

Rather than back down entirely (too passive) or respond with violence (too aggressive), the emotionally intelligent response would be to look for a compromise. "No" is not very helpful if someone needs help. But saying "No, but ..." demonstrates that you are willing to be flexible. Show that you are prepared to accept part of the individual's request in return for having some of your needs met.

Some ideas for finding a workable middle ground:

- *Create a time out.* If you can, be upfront and ask for a break. Explain that the situation is not being resolved and you think that a break might help both of you to think more clearly. But do emphasize that this is your feeling – "I feel that we're not getting anywhere – can we take a break?" rather than "We're not getting anywhere." However, if emotions are running high and you judge that the other person will not voluntarily allow you one – invent a reason to create a time out. You need a glass of water, a toilet break, a cigarette, or to answer an urgent phone call.
- *Establish your wants versus your needs.* Your wants are what you ideally want to get out of the situation, whereas your needs are what you would be willing to

accept as a bare minimum. Often we begin discussions by asserting our wants as opposed to our needs. But accepting a solution that still allows you to meet your needs as opposed to your wish list of wants may be enough of a compromise to satisfy both of you.

- *Generate alternatives.* Thinking about your wants versus your needs, try to identify other options for taking the discussion forward. If you aren't able to come into the office all weekend, would you be willing to take some work home or come in on Saturday morning or Sunday evening? If you can't attend a particular meeting, could you contribute after the meeting or attend a later meeting in their stead?
- *Use "If... then ..." statements to suggest your alternatives.* "If you could find someone to cover Saturday, then I could cover Sunday." "If I were to spend a month training someone, then would you let me take the secondment?"

The difficulty of negotiating is not in choosing the right words. Choosing the right words is a skill that most intelligent people can do. The difficulty comes in managing your emotions and those of your counterpart – and that requires emotional intelligence.

Communicate without words

They say that actions speak louder than words. And a psychologist by the suitably professorial name of Albert Mehrabian has established that the gestures, movements, and expressions that make up our body language account for 55 percent of our communication effectiveness. Another 38 percent comes from the tone of our voice. And only a paltry 7 percent comes from the actual words that we use.

We have already discussed reading other people's body language to understand the messages they may be sending. But we can also use body language to influence other people without their noticing through a technique called "mirroring" – or matching our non-verbal cues to those of others to build more effective rapport.

When you want to accelerate rapport, try to observe someone's overall level of activity. Are they almost motionless or constantly moving, shifting position, and using gestures? Then try to match that person's overall behavior by dampening or injecting more energy into your natural activity levels.

As a meeting progresses, look out for more subtle non-verbal cues:

- *Watch your posture.* If someone sits very upright in their chair, then sitting in a slouched manner would draw attention to your body language for the wrong reasons. On the other hand, if that person slouches, you should slouch.

- *Use appropriate gestures.* People vary in the extent to which they gesticulate and illustrate their words with their hands. If they use their hands a lot, then try to think of appropriate gestures to describe what you are saying. What would you do with your hands when you say, for instance, "huge" or "no" or "excited" or "awful"?

- *Match their facial expressiveness.* If they are very expressive, nodding and shaking their heads, frowning and smiling, then you should follow suit.

Effective mirroring is about matching overall body language patterns. In simple terms, if they do a lot of something, you do a lot of it too; if they don't do it much, you don't either. But it needs to be subtle and unobtrusive. While the technique is called mirroring, the aim is not to form a literal mirror by copying their every gesture and movement. If you were to scratch your head or cross and uncross your arms every time they did the same, they will almost certainly interpret your efforts as mockery of their mannerisms. Bang, there goes the rapport.

Mind your language

While body language makes up the biggest chunk of your impact on others, don't forget that your words and voice make up over 40 percent too. People tend to like people like themselves, so matching your words and voice will speed the rapport building process too.

There are levels to matching your words and voice. The easiest way to begin is to listen to the words and language that are being used around you. I'm sure you are bright enough to have noticed not to swear when others aren't swearing. On the other hand when I have, for example, run a meeting in a shop floor environment, then not swearing often marks you out as someone different, an interloper not to be trusted.

The use or avoidance of jargon can help you to blend in with others too. Don't you hate it when people use words and phrases of jargon that are unintelligible to anyone outside their field? The sad truth is that so many people do it – and all without realizing their impact on others. But as an emotionally intelligent person, you should know better.

Matching pace and tone require more effort on your part to be effective. If they are speaking quickly and excitably, then infuse your voice with more energy. Or if they are measured and thoughtful, pausing between sentences, then you should try to slow down to match their pace. A good trick for forcing yourself to slow down is to swallow between sentences.

The most difficult method of building rapport through words and voice is to adapt your speech patterns. Listen out for their level of enunciation and try to match it. As a personal example, despite having been to good schools, I tend to say "yeah" instead of "yes." But when I am with a client with blue blood shooting through their veins, I damn well make sure that I say "yes" rather than "yeah."

However, I am most certainly not suggesting that you adopt an American accent with your client from New York or an Indian accent with a colleague from Mumbai, because it won't work. In fact, it is a guaranteed method of offending them. Game over "dude!"

BUILDING REWARDING RELATIONSHIPS

Communicating effectively allows you to tell other people what you want and need. Communicating well enables you to issue clear instructions and make requests that others cannot fail to understand. The only problem is that people can still choose to ignore you. Maybe they have more pressing matters or perhaps they just cannot be bothered to help you. After all, what's in it for them?

Building rapport through empathy is a start to the relationship building process. But it is very much only a start. You can have a great rapport with someone that you encounter at a client meeting or a party one evening. But you wouldn't expect them to put themselves out for you based only on that tiny shred of rapport.

The key to influencing people successfully is to build strong enough relationships with them that you start to matter to them. If you become an important part of their lives – an ally, a confidant, a friend – then why wouldn't they want to help you out in any way they can?

And you can build rewarding relationships by:

- responding and reciprocating;
- understanding innermost needs;
- respecting relationship boundaries;
- building other-esteem;
- controlling emotional outbursts;
- facilitating problem-solving;
- seeing the glass as half full.

Respond and reciprocate

Let's take relationships out of the workplace for a moment. Have you ever been in a relationship in which you had to do all the hard work? Either with a friend, a flatmate, or a significant other, did you have to pick up the phone more frequently, or pay for everything, or do more housework, or initiate sex more of the time? If you have, then you will know that it gets tiresome very quickly. Because successful relationships are based on reciprocity – the desire to meet each other's wants and needs.

Satisfying relationships at work are based on reciprocity too. You ask them for help, and in turn they ask you for help. If one party is putting in more time and effort, then the relationship becomes unbalanced. Think about your colleagues who come to you for practical assistance or emotional support. At first it can be flattering to be asked for help, but it soon becomes wearing. And of course the same goes for people that you need a lot of help from too – you are probably reluctant to go to them again because you know that there is a one-way flow of support rather than an exchange.

In order to build useful relationships at work, you must ensure that you respond to requests for help at least as often as you make requests. It's even better if you can provide slightly more support than you require from others – as this will put you in a good position should you ever need their help or support on a major issue or problem of yours. Help them, but remember that a relationship exists between only two people – be humble and avoid broadcasting your generosity to others.

But reciprocity is about more than merely responding to the requests that people make of you. Unlike an emotionally intelligent person such as yourself, other people often have unexpressed needs that they may be too shy, embarrassed, or cautious to mention. Your job is to discover these needs. If you can discover them and work towards meeting them, then you can win them over. And influencing them in the future will be no work at all.

The most straightforward way to establish another person's needs is to ask them. One of the best times to ask is when you have just received some form of help from them. Start by thanking them and then ask how you could return the favor. "That is such a help – thanks for that. What could I ever do to return the favor?" Many people will brush the question aside. They might never have considered what you could do for them, or they might not be used to articulating their needs to other people. Or they may believe that politeness requires them to say, "Nothing." But here is where a little persistence can pay off. "Honestly, I'd like to be able to help. What could I do for you?" If they continue to say that they don't have any needs, you could make some suggestions. "Well, I'm good with spreadsheets, or if you ever need someone to proofread a document, I'd be happy to help."

Be gentle asking about how you could help, though, as people may feel vulnerable talking about their needs. Don't expect everybody to divulge all of their needs the first time you meet them. Building a relationship takes time. They may not tell you their needs the first or second, fifth, or tenth time – but they will eventually.

Understand innermost needs

A long time ago in a galaxy far, far away, I used to work in a consulting firm that was run by two partners. Matthew ran a change management team while the other partner ran an assessment team. The assessment team made lots of money while Matthew's team struggled and in fact lost money. But Matthew refused to retrain his team to become assessment consultants, even though that would have made him much more money. Why? He never said it out loud, but it was because he didn't want to be subordinate to the other partner. He needed to feel in control and to be seen by people outside of the company as a leader and an equal partner. Recognition was more important than money. And when I realized that, it became child's play to manage Matthew.

People never talk about their innermost needs. Emotionally unintelligent folk are probably entirely unaware of what actually drives them to behave the way they do. Others are afraid to discuss their private drivers because they fear it might give away the means of controlling them.

And for that very reason, you should use all of your listening, observation, and empathy skills to try to understand people's innermost needs.

There are all sorts of models of motivation by theorists such as Frederick Herzberg, Abraham Maslow, and David McClelland. But I shall resist the urge to bore you with the theories and instead cut to the chase and talk about some of the commonest needs instead:

- *Money.* The song from the musical *Cabaret* proclaims: "Money makes the world go around." But for many people, even if they say that they are driven by money, they may not be entirely telling the whole truth. Very few people actually want money for its own sake. Many people actually seek money because it provides security for themselves or their families. Others believe that amassing it is a vindication of their abilities or recognition of their worth.

- *Recognition.* People like my ex-boss Matthew crave recognition. They want status and seek to gain respect from colleagues or friends. Recognition allows them to feel good about themselves. Perhaps they feel inadequate without recognition – ever heard the phrase "chip on the shoulder"? Giving these people your attention, praise, and compliments is the way to satisfy their innermost need.

- *Control.* Everyone likes to feel in control of their own lives. But some people enjoy having power and influence over others too. They need to be in control of teams, departments, or entire organizations. Giving these people the opportunity to take charge makes them feel good about themselves.

- *Social contact.* Different people require different levels of social contact. Think about the people that you work with – some are happy to sit at their desks and get on with their work while others are like butterflies, needing to flit from desk to desk to chat and regale others with their stories and humor. When people need social contact or to feel part of a team, they can often be satisfied by simply always remembering to ask them if they would like to be included in activities.

- *Personal growth.* These sorts of people thrive on having new challenges, accomplishing difficult tasks, succeeding at overcoming obstacles, and bettering themselves. Emphasizing the difficulty of the task at hand and the learning that it will afford them is often a good way to persuade them to work harder.

- *An easy life.* There are some people who – perhaps it's a mix of being emotionally unintelligent as well as a bit classically unintelligent – want only an easy life. They want a job that pays them enough and gives them as little stress as possible. They want to arrive at nine o'clock and leave at five o'clock. They won't tend to be movers and shakers, and it's best to avoid these people if you possibly can.

Those are some of the most common innermost needs. But the reality is that human beings can be astoundingly complex. So don't expect the people you encounter to have only a single innermost need. Some people have several. Furthermore, we change our minds. The death of a loved one, the break-up of a relationship, the arrival of children in our lives, or simply the passing of time and greater maturity – all of these can and do change our innermost needs. But if you can delve below the surface of what people say in order to understand these unspoken needs, you will be able to befriend them and keep them on your side in the workplace.

Respect relationship boundaries

The first time I met a particular executive – a finance manager in an insurance business – she came up to me and, clasping both of my hands in hers, kissed me on both cheeks. I was slightly stunned. I have no problem greeting friends with kisses, but this encounter felt wrong. It had breached an unwritten code of contact – that you shake hands on first meeting someone. Sure, I know that people in creative industries such as fashion and media greet each other with kisses. But in an insurance company? It felt over-familiar. She had overstepped the boundaries of our working relationship.

Relationship boundaries are unspoken rules that guide how two parties in a relationship behave with each other. The only time the rules are usually noticed is when one party oversteps them. As an emotionally intelligent individual, you should aim to identify and abide by them, while at the same time looking for new ways to extend the unspoken boundaries and deepen the relationship. Keep in mind possible boundaries around:

- *The type of help that is required.* For instance, one colleague may value you for the practical assistance you provide when she is busy, while another may value you more for listening to his personal problems than in helping with his workload. Neither person will mention these rules, but identifying them will help you to navigate the relationships successfully.
- *Topics of conversation that are taboo.* For example, some colleagues feel that emotions are best left at home

while others might happily discuss their personal relationships and sex lives. Or a customer might be happy only to discuss their company's goals and successes but not their mistakes and failures.

- *Methods and timings of contact.* You might put up with your boss interrupting your work throughout the working day, but how would you feel about a phone call in the evening or even "dropping by" to visit you on a weekend? Keep in mind that different people have very different definitions of acceptable boundaries around methods of contact. For example, some colleagues may prefer to be contacted by email, viewing phone calls or face-to-face meetings as irritating intrusions.

- *Frequency of contact.* How often does your boss check up on you? Or how often do you check up on your team? Daily or weekly or not at all? How often do you call your customers? Some might deem once a week too much, while another might think a single call every week is not enough. Tailor your frequency of contact to the needs of each individual.

Be vigilant not to assume greater levels of intimacy than other people are prepared to accept. Tailor your approach to each person. Ask them how much is enough or too much. Invite them to talk about new topics, but then back off if they seem unduly uncomfortable.

Your ultimate aim is to extend the boundaries and deepen the relationship, as it will cement the relationship and allow you to influence them more easily in the future. Whenever there seems a mismatch between their words and body language – for example when someone claims to be "fine" but seems upset about something – ask if you can help. "I hope I'm not intruding but I can't help feeling that there's something bothering you – want to talk about it?" or "Stop me if I'm prying, but you seem upset." If you deal with each other mainly by telephone, you could try "I just realized that we always speak by phone – maybe we should meet for a coffee sometime?" Or if you would like to speak more frequently, say so: "I can't help thinking that two weeks is a long time to wait before I check up on this issue. Would you mind if I gave you a call later this week to see if everything is going well?"

However, extending relationship boundaries happens slowly over time and is a process of trial and error. Relationships are not deepened in a day. Be sensitive in making your suggestion, and be prepared for people to say "no" on several occasions before they open up to you.

Build other-esteem

If you have ever had a good idea of yours rubbished by another person, then you will know how important it is to build other-esteem. Other-esteem is shorthand for "other people's self-esteem," and building it is basically the psychobabble term for making other people feel confident and good about themselves. The workplace is full of put-downs, unwarranted criticism, and disparagement that are guaranteed to destroy other-esteem. When was the last time you heard someone storm round the office complaining that they were sick of receiving praise, compliments, or recognition?

In fact the opposite is true. Surveys repeatedly show that the vast majority of people feel undervalued – that they do not receive enough recognition for their efforts. And, interestingly enough, the most frequently cited reason for changing jobs isn't to go for a pay rise, but to join a team where they feel more valued for their efforts.

Instilling confidence in others can have miraculous effects. Earlier this year, a researcher found that giving power lifters – big hulking national standard athletes – a sugar pill but telling them that it was a steroid helped them to lift 5 percent more than their personal bests. When the same group of lifters were told that they were being given a sugar pill, it made their performance worse. Confidence can literally make people better than they have ever been.

Everyone has highs and lows. And helping others through their lows to feel good about themselves will make them rally round you when you need help.

As a rule of thumb: acknowledge good efforts; praise good results.

Perhaps a bit more explanation will help to bring the adage to life. If someone puts a lot of time and effort into a task or project, they deserve acknowledgement for it – even if they perhaps did not get the results they were hoping for. They may be feeling frustrated, so providing a few simple words of recognition of their efforts will help to lift them from their disappointment more quickly. On the other hand, feel free to offer unmitigated praise when others work hard and achieve good results.

Some tips for providing effective praise:

- *Praise only when it is warranted.* Praising for its own sake cheapens the currency.
- *Praise consistently across the team.* While criticism should always be delivered one on one, success is often celebrated publicly. If you single one person out for his or her achievement, ensure that the reasons are clear so that others do not perceive you to have favorites.
- *Say what was good and go on to explain how or why it was good.* Saying "great proposal" is not particularly helpful. Just as negative feedback needs to be specific to be useful, positive feedback needs to be specific too – "great proposal, the client thought it was well laid out and informative without being verbose."
- *Separate praise from constructive criticism.* If you want to congratulate someone but also need to talk about how someone could have worked more effectively, save it for a separate occasion. Otherwise the praise will sound merely like a shallow attempt to soften the blow in the lead up to criticism.

However, insincere compliments are worse than none at all. I used to work with a senior colleague who was particularly bad at this. Even though she would curl her mouth into a smile when saying, "That's a great idea Rob," I could always tell from her eyes and the inflection in her voice that she was really thinking, "That's a stupid idea but

I feel the need to say something positive about poor Rob." A simple "No, that won't work" would have sufficed. If I ever need to patronize or put someone down, then I try to summon up the special way that she used to do it.

Control emotional outbursts

In attempting to build rewarding relationships with people, it helps to be able to offer them practical assistance when they are faced with a problem or a crisis. But what do most people do in a crisis? They panic or worry or get angry – they get emotional. And what should they be doing? They should be staying calm and rational. Accordingly, you may need to help them to control their emotions before you can help them to solve their problem.

However, simply telling people to relax or calm down usually has the exact opposite effect – they usually become even more incensed or agitated.

You should now appreciate that the techniques you use to manage your own negative thoughts and physical sensations can be adapted to control emotional outbursts in other people too. In fact, the key to being able to help them to solve their problem often depends on helping them to manage their physical agitation first. Typically, when the physical agitation subsides, the problem becomes far less daunting.

Begin by telling the individual that you want to hear what the matter is. But tell them that they need to slow down so that you can understand them properly. If you need to, take them aside so that the two of you can speak candidly without having to worry about other people overhearing you.

The next three steps are a combination of activities designed to tackle their physical agitation. First, suggest that they sit down (it will help to calm muscular tension). Second, ask them to speak more slowly (it will help to slow their breathing). Then third, offer to fetch a drink (it will alleviate a dry mouth, yet another physical sensation associated with emotional distress). There is method behind the terribly British madness of having a cup of tea in a crisis!

As their physical agitation continues to subside, ask them to tell you slowly and clearly what the problem is. Keep in mind the difference between using questions sensitively to encourage talking, and forcing someone to talk – a difference often rendered in the tone and pace of your voice. Then listen, using your summarizing and paraphrasing skills to slow the conversation even further.

Most importantly, the key here is to empathize and validate their emotions to demonstrate that you are not fazed by their show of emotion – perhaps with phrases such as "I understand how you feel" and "No wonder you seem upset." And once their physical agitation is under control and you have listened to their situation, you can attempt to challenge their automatic negative thoughts (ANTs). They may be repeating phrases such as:

- "I can't ..."
- "I've never been any good at ..."
- "They never give me a chance to ..."
- "He is always so spiteful/unfair/negative, etcetera."

Challenge ANTs about themselves by contradicting them – "Yes you can do it." Challenge ANTs about third parties involved in this situation by asking questions such as: "Is he really nasty to you all of the time?"

Each time they repeat a negative assertion about themselves or another person, challenge it. And keep challenging gently until they see that there might be an alternative interpretation to their situation. You will know that you have succeeded when they finally acknowledge that they might be able to cope with the situation, or that the third party might not be as completely nasty as they had first thought.

Facilitate problem-solving

Do you have any bad habits? Perhaps you eat, drink, or smoke too much, or exercise too little. Or maybe you drive too fast or sunbathe more often than you should. Now think back to the last time someone told you off for your bad habits – how you should be living your life. How did that feel? Did their advice convince you to change your life? I don't know about you, but I tend to find it high-minded and patronizing.

And in the same way that you don't respond to advice about your lifestyle, people at work often don't respond to advice about their problems. People hate being told what they should do. Even if your advice is sound – or in the case of smoking, eating, and drinking too much, backed up by decades of research – others may reject it because they subconsciously resent being told what to do.

Helping people to tackle their problems will win you their respect. But because giving advice rarely works – even once you have controlled their emotions – the more successful way to help is to ask insightful questions that will allow others to come up with their own solutions. These questions come in three phases:

1. Open questions to establish the situation.
2. Open questions to identify and evaluate options.
3. Closed questions to narrow down options.

The first step is to ask further questions to establish the rest of the facts that you may not have. (Remember that you asked some questions as part of the tactics to control the emotional outburst.) What has caused the current problem or crisis? If other people are involved, what have they said or done? What has happened in the run-up to the situation? Your task here is to help the individual to consider all of the relevant information rather than rush into a hasty and wrong decision. You need to help them to focus on how to tackle the root problem rather than merely one of the possibly many symptoms.

Secondly, use further questions to help the individual to consider and evaluate options for dealing with the situation. When you begin to discuss options, start with open-ended questions such as:

- "What do you think you could do about that?"
- "How else could you deal with that?"
- "What do you think other people might do in this situation?"

Keep asking mainly "what" questions to generate a number of options. Essentially, you are helping them to brainstorm – without mentioning that it is brainstorming. If they struggle to come up with any ideas, then you could suggest some – "I don't know if this would work, but what if we tried...."

As the discussion progresses, introduce questions that will help them to evaluate the costs benefits of their different options. Ensure that your questions are phrased in a sensitive way and are not at all interrogative. For example, try:

- "How do you think they would react to that idea?"
- "That's a good idea but how much time/ money/effort would it take to do that?"
- "Do you think that would be better received than your other suggestion?"

In an ideal situation, with more questions and considerable patience on your part, the individual should be able to identify a solution that works for them. In reality, an individual may answer your questions with "I don't know" or may simply give up. This is when you should move into the third step – asking more directional or closed questions to steer their thinking:

- "Do you think that they would realistically allow you to do that?"
- "I think I can see why you say that, but what do you think is the likelihood of that happening?"
- "Would that not upset him even more?"

As you can see, closed questions allow you to put your opinions across too. But always begin with open questions with the aim of helping people to reach their own conclusions.

When facilitating problem-solving, remember to adopt a supportive tone of voice and to intersperse your questions with active listening, empathy, and good paraphrasing and summarizing. Firing questions in rapid succession could easily make your discussion seem like a cross-examination rather than an attempt to help.

Once the individual has identified a course of action, help them think about how to turn it into a SMART goal. Because, as we know, a SMART goal is much more likely to effect a real change and tackle the problem than a vague one.

See the glass as half full

I used to work with a colleague who was always having a bad time at work. Every time we saw him, my office mate and I took bets on whether he would be having a bad day. And, more often than not, he was. If it wasn't complaints about his team or the politics, it was the stress he was under and how much he wanted to leave the company. Moan, moan, moan. But the sad truth was that he wasn't remotely aware of his tendency to talk himself down. He was a liability to himself. And the rest of us would only work with him reluctantly.

No one likes to hear people whine about their jobs all the time. You can probably think of the people in your own office who act like little black holes – sucking any pleasant feelings from the room with their despondency. So try to keep your feelings to yourself. Moods are infectious, and any negativity you express will bring others down too.

Instead, try to act optimistic. Even if you don't feel optimistic, you should try to behave as if you do. Be positive about your work and the future. Be grateful about what you do have rather than focusing on what you lack.

Do it because your behavior will boost the mood of the people around you. It will get you noticed. All other things being equal, who do you think the organization would rather promote – the optimist or the pessimist? And – remembering that connection between your behavior and your own mood – the more positively you behave, the more quickly you will be able to turn your own mood around too.

Now I'm not suggesting that you ignore the really bad stuff when it happens. When the organization has to make people redundant or if a project goes badly wrong, it's OK to discuss it.

Neither am I suggesting that you skip into the office every day, beaming at everyone and pretending that life is perfect. But perhaps you could monitor any comments you feel like making about the more minor gripes at work. Yes, sometimes it can feel good to make them. On the other hand, if you want to make a good impression on your colleagues or your boss, could you possibly not say them?

TACKLING UNSATISFACTORY RELATIONSHIPS

Despite our best intentions, we don't always have fulfilling and mutually beneficial relationships with everyone that we encounter.

Often we do not like other people because they do not like us. There can be all manner of reasons why they may not like us. They may think that we are too different in terms of personality or background, values or goals. They may not like us because of our gender, age, ethnicity, sexuality, or religion. They may even be jealous of our success. Or we may have said or done something to offend them inadvertently.

People who do not like you can be obstructive and disruptive in many ways. They might be overtly difficult – arguing with you and criticizing you, or making malicious comments about you behind your back. Or if they are not being blatantly hostile, they can resist you in a myriad of subtle ways – "forgetting" to relay messages, deleting your emails "by mistake," or always leaving your work until the last possible moment.

The following steps will help you to tackle unsatisfactory relationships:

- broaching disagreements;
- discussing differences;
- acknowledging personality differences;
- respecting personality differences;
- establishing ground rules;
- restoring goodwill;
- acting as a peacemaker.

Some experts would argue that it is important to cultivate rewarding relationships with everyone. My view is that life is too short to attempt to salvage every broken relationship. In some cases, it may be wise simply to avoid the people you don't get on with. However, if someone is either affecting your ability to do your job or causing you undue grief, you may find it necessary to grit your teeth and tackle them, bearing in mind that the short-term pain of confronting them should realize long-term gains.

Broach disagreements

Years ago, I worked with an office manager who hated me. She would arrive in the mornings and say "Good morning" only if I said it first. If there were no one else in the room, she would sometimes avoid speaking to me at all. I have to admit that the feeling was fairly mutual – she hated me, and I came to hate her too. Unfortunately, we had to work together.

The problem could have worsened, but one day I confided in my boss, who suggested that I talk to the office manager. When I did talk to her, we had a huge argument. There were accusations and lots of anger, denial, and defensiveness on both sides. But somehow we were both able to blurt out what we each thought the other had done wrong. Miraculously, it cleared the air and over the course of several months, an uneasy truce turned into a comfortable working relationship.

I am not suggesting that having a violent argument with someone is the best way to tackle a difficult relationship. Indeed, the opposite is true – a discussion needs to be as calm as possible. But the important point is that you need to initiate the discussion. Relationships do not repair themselves on their own. It takes one of the two parties (in other words, you) to be brave and broach the matter.

Some tips for preparing to broach the difficult topic of a relationship breakdown with an individual:

- *Ask for a second opinion.* Rather than rushing into a confrontation, ask a trusted colleague who knows you both for their thoughts on the situation. It is natural to believe that the other party is completely at fault. But when it comes to interpersonal differences, remember that different people can interpret the same situation in completely opposite ways – and it could possibly be your interpretation that is slightly skewed or even wrong.

- *Try to act sooner rather than later.* Otherwise people eventually forget the original cause of a spat or disagreement, but the resentment and ill-feeling only grow worse as time goes by.

- *Approach the other individual only when you feel completely calm and in control of your emotions.* Repeating positive affirmations such as, "I will stay calm; I will stay in control of my emotions" may create the right state of mind.

- *Choose the right time and place.* "I wonder if we could meet later to discuss an issue that has been bothering me." Resist the urge to discuss it then and there. Perhaps suggest to the individual that you want to meet for a coffee or lunch away from the workplace and the prying eyes and ears of other colleagues. At a minimum, find an office with thick walls.

- *Be conciliatory in both your verbal and non-verbal communication when you broach the topic.* Speak quietly and slowly. Ensure that your body language is open too – for example with your palms upturned in supplication rather than clenched into fists.
- Stay calm throughout the discussion. Use all of your self-awareness skills to monitor your emotions. For example, pay attention to physical sensations and symptoms and dampen them down. And ask to take a time out if necessary if you can feel your emotions boiling up.

Now you have broached the topic, you are ready to discuss your differences.

Discuss differences

Emotions are likely to run high during any attempt to discuss interpersonal differences, so it is imperative that you choose the right words to avoid provoking the other person. A poorly chosen word or turn of phrase can easily sound accusatory.

Some steps as follows:

- *Introduce the topic.* Explain that you sense some tension between the two of you and that you want to clear it up. Use phrases such as "I get the feeling that we aren't getting on," or "I feel that there has been a bit of a breakdown in communication."

- *Emphasize that you want only to relate your side of the disagreement.* Remember that you can only comment on your perception of what has happened. Their perception might be (and usually is) completely different. "I realize that there are two sides to the story, so all I want to do is share with you some of my observations and thoughts and see what you think."
- *Get their input early.* Rather than launching immediately into criticism of them, ask them what they think. "How do you think we have been getting on?" or "Have I said or done anything to offend you at all?"
- *Persist, persist, persist.* Often the other person may say that nothing is wrong because they feel too embarrassed or annoyed to want to talk. They may suspect that you have a hidden agenda. So repeat the question in different ways to get them talking.

When you talk about your perceptions, continue to make it very clear that these are your feelings or interpretations by talking about the issues in the first person (by saying "I") rather than in the second person ("you"). Avoid labeling other people when all you can legitimately do is label your own emotions and explain your interpretation of events.

In many cases, "you" statements are wrong because they imply that you know what the other person's intentions are; the reality is that you cannot know for certain what they had in mind. For example, saying "You always avoid me when you walk past me" is a poor statement because you cannot know for certain what the other person's intentions are. The other person could counter your claim by saying that they are merely preoccupied with other thoughts and forget to acknowledge you. As such, it is better to explain your perception of their behavior: "I often feel that you are ignoring me."

As another example, saying "You exclude me from meetings" sounds as if you are accusing them of deliberately excluding you from meetings. Such a claim is almost certain to provoke anger or at least irritation. It would be better to say, "I'm not being invited to all of the team's meetings."

"You make me feel" is another inaccuracy. It implies that other people can control your feelings. But in actuality it is your interpretation of their behavior that makes you feel a particular way. So it would be better to say to someone that when they do something, "It makes me feel...."

Provide evidence based on what you have seen or heard. Avoid saying "You were angry with me" when you cannot know with complete certainty what emotion they were experiencing. It may be the case that they raised their voice and threw your document across your desk, but it could be that the other person believed that he or she was actually being completely reasonable (!) – so quote the evidence that you saw instead: "I felt you were getting angry when you raised your voice and threw the document across my desk."

Throughout the discussion, give the other person an opportunity to respond. The more you can encourage them to talk, the more likely you will be to establish the underlying cause of the disagreement and find a way to resolve it.

Acknowledge personality differences

One of the many differences between my office manager and me that caused us to argue was in how we preferred to communicate with each other. When I asked her to arrange a meeting, for example, I thought I was helping her out by leaving detailed instructions for her by email, whereas it turned out that she preferred to talk to people in person. So she thought that I was avoiding her by using email.

Sometimes we clash with other people because of fundamental differences in our personal styles. Accordingly some knowledge of personality differences may help you to understand why a relationship isn't working.

Originally derived from Jungian theory, the Myers–Briggs Type Indicator (MBTI) is one of the world's most commonly used personality tests. You don't need to understand the theory behind it. But having a basic appreciation of its four dimensions will help you to analyze why some of your relationships may be exasperating or unproductive.

While there are no "right" or "wrong" personality types, people who are opposite types frequently find each other difficult to work with. But if you find someone frustrating to work with because their personality type differs from your own, bear in mind that they probably have the same sentiment about you too. However, if you know your type and can identify another person's type, you may be able to adapt your behavior to suit them or discuss with them ways to work together.

In order to use the MBTI model to enhance your understanding of a difficult individual, begin by identifying your own type from the descriptions below. Then observe the individual closely and take mental note of how they behave. Read through the brief descriptions and try to match the descriptions against each type. If you find that neither type describes them very well, it is entirely possible that they sit in the middle of the scale. However, if you can fit them into any of the types, it will help you to come up with ideas on how to tackle your differences.

Respect personality differences

The following descriptions try to summarize what is usually described in hefty manuals and weighty tomes. However, even these brief summaries should allow you to deepen your emotional intelligence by understanding the basics of personality differences. As you read through them, think about whether any of the dimensions could describe any of the people that you find it difficult to deal with.

The first dimension measures extraversion versus introversion. Unlike the popular use of the terms, extraversion and introversion in the Myers–Briggs framework do not refer to whether you have social skills or not. They refer instead to whether you prefer to process ideas outside of your head by discussing them with other people (extraversion) or inside of your head by thinking them over by yourself (introversion). Some tips for each type:

- Extraverts – are outspoken in meetings and typically want to talk everything through with other people. When working by themselves, they find it difficult to come up with new ideas and tend to get bored quickly. They tend to find introverts cold and unfriendly.

- Introverts – prefer to work through tasks and problems on their own. If you give an introvert a task or problem to solve, they would much rather take it away and think about it before giving you an answer. They find it difficult to concentrate with people around them. They tend to find extraverts too talkative and pushy.

The intuition/sensing dimension measures the way that people like to take in information. Sensing types are grounded in facts and reality – they prefer to gather information through their five senses, looking for practical solutions based on past experience of what has or has not worked. Intuitive types look for patterns and associations between facts as opposed to looking at facts themselves – one could say that they rely on their sixth sense of intuition rather than their five senses.

- Sensing types – prefer to deal with facts and details. They are good at dealing with immediate problems but tend to struggle with long-term thinking or untested ideas. They tend to be good at following rules and procedures, and can be relied upon to come up with practical solutions. They tend to find intuitive types too abstract and insufficiently grounded in reality.
- Intuitive types – enjoy dealing with concepts, theories, and "big picture" thinking. They are good at long-term thinking but get bored with short-term plans and detail. They shy away from following procedures and prefer to focus on new ideas or solutions. They tend to find sensing types boring and unimaginative.

The dimension of thinking/feeling describes the way that individuals like to make decisions. Thinking types tend to evaluate choices logically, weighing up the pros and cons in coming to a decision. Feeling types tend to evaluate choices based on a personal code of values – they are more interested in how different decisions make them (and others) feel.

- Thinking types – are good at seeing flaws in an argument and playing 'devil's advocate'. They tend to have strong analytical skills and often have strong views on right and wrong, taking a fairly black and white view of the world. They find feeling types irrational and overly concerned with feelings and emotions.

- Feeling types – are good at seeing the benefits of different arguments and encouraging cooperation between different parties. They are less preoccupied with logical analysis of right and wrong, and more interested in finding a solution that meets the needs of the people affected by a decision. They find thinking types unfeeling and tactless.

The judging/perceiving dimension assesses how people like to deal with the external world. Judging types like to have an orderly existence – they value decisiveness and like to be highly organized. They get satisfaction from closure and completing tasks. On the other hand, perceiving types like to have spontaneous, flexible lives – they dislike having to make decisions that could later limit their options. They get satisfaction from keeping opportunities open.

- Judging types – are good planners and organizers. They enjoy making decisions, taking charge in a crisis, and persisting until a task is completed. However, they tend to be inflexible and sometimes make decisions too quickly. They find perceiving types disorganized and poor decision makers.
- Perceiving types – are good at brainstorming and generating ideas and options. They adapt well to changing circumstances and work best under last-minute time pressure. However, they may not complete tasks that they start and sometimes procrastinate. They find judging types inflexible and overly hasty decision makers.

Having read those descriptions, which type do you fall into? For example, I'm an introvert–sensing– thinking–judging type. I differed on three out of the four dimensions with my office manager who was an extravert–intuitive–feeling–judging type. Now try to apply your understanding of the MBTI to your relationships.

Establish ground rules

Sometimes the mere fact that you have discussed your differences will be enough to restore some measure of a working relationship. However, it often helps to be more explicit about how you each want the other to behave in order to ensure that the newly repaired relationship does not break down again.

The best way to establish some ground rules is to talk explicitly about it:

- *Explain that you want to ensure that the two of you do not clash in the future again.* Suggest to the other person that you would like to discuss some ground rules to guide both of your behavior in the future. Ask them if they think it would be a good idea – get their agreement before setting ground rules.
- *Ask them how they would like you to behave in future.* Ask them what they need from you and why. If you think that any of their needs are unreasonable, explain why.
- *When they have told you some of their needs, go on to suggest some of your needs.* And explain why each of your needs is important – remember that telling someone what you need is fairly ineffective without explaining why you need it too.
- *Expect to have to compromise.* If you find that some of their needs are unrealistic or overly demanding, you may need to give and take. What are you willing to give up or agree to in order to find a solution?
- *Keep the tone of the discussion open and honest.* Keep studying not only your own verbal and non-verbal cues but also theirs. This is not a hostile negotiation and if any emotions creep in on either side, you may need to take steps to curb them.
- *At the end of the discussion, you both need to be happy with the ground rules.* Ask the other person if they are satisfied. If they feel at all resentful or put out by the ground rules, then you need to discuss further. If you do not, then the likelihood is that the ground rules will be a waste of breath.

If you believe that a particular relationship is very important but at the same time rather tenuous, you may want to introduce a little more formality into your agreement. I'm not suggesting a legal contract, but I know that writing down a few ground rules – even if only in an email – helps some people to ensure that both parties know what is expected of them.

Restore goodwill

Discussing differences helps to clear up misunderstandings and misinterpretations. However, even when the differences have been discussed and new ground rules agreed, both parties can still experience lingering feelings of resentment. Out of you and the other person, guess whose job it is to deal with that resentment?

Accepting your mistakes and apologizing for them is a powerful technique for salvaging goodwill. Even if you did not intend to cause offence, you should be able to acknowledge that the other person may have perceived your behavior as upsetting. Your apology does not need to be excessive or overly profuse, but it does have to be sincere.

However, be careful not to fall into the trap of mock apologizing. Many people find it difficult to apologize and end up saying, "Sorry, but ..." which makes the apology another attempt to justify their behavior rather than a genuine attempt to convey regret.

Another technique for restoring goodwill is to look for mutual common ground between you and the other person. People like people like themselves. Psychologists call this "congruence" – the fact that people warm to people who have similar interests, goals, and values. Look for commonalities between you and the other person, and scatter them into your discussion. For example:

- "We both want to do what's in the best interests of the business."
- "I guess we can both be fairly headstrong people."
- "We both want to produce good-quality work."

But be careful not to make invalid assumptions. If the other person has not said as much, then you cannot claim to know what they are thinking or feeling. If you are making assumptions, then at least clarify that fact, for example: "I'm assuming that neither of us wants to fight about this any more" or "My assumption is that we both understand each other now."

Finally, try to end on a high note. Show your appreciation by thanking the other person for having listened to you and giving you the opportunity to express your concerns. A simple "Thank you for agreeing to this discussion," said sincerely, can be the perfect way to finish any difficult discussion.

Act as a peacemaker

Now that you understand how to handle conflict when it affects yourself, you can try to apply the same skill to resolve tricky situations involving other people. Acting as a mediator and diplomat will earn you respect, as people come to realize that you can defuse situations that they can't sort out for themselves.

Consider carefully when to intervene and when not to, though. Your attempts to act as a peacemaker could easily be seen as an unwelcome intrusion. If you are present in a meeting when two parties have an argument, then your involvement may well be warranted. Or if a dispute between two parties is affecting your or the team's ability to do the job, then you may also need to intervene. In other situations that do not directly affect you, be extremely careful, as the warring individuals could easily decide to turn their anger and frustration on you for daring to interfere.

We have already covered the key skills of being an effective peacemaker: listening, asking insightful questions, and paraphrasing and summarizing. However, here are some further tips on how to apply them to moderating disputes between two parties:

- *Dampen down their emotions first.* People cannot have a productive discussion if they are feeling angry or upset. Encourage both parties to move to a quiet room away from other colleagues and get them to sit down. Try to delay letting them speak, or at least slow them both down, as it will reduce any physical sensations and symptoms that could contribute to strong emotions.
- *Ask questions of both parties.* Try to establish the situation and the background that has led up to the disagreement. Try to ascertain the facts. What happened? How did it happen? How does it affect each party? If the two parties refuse to talk to each other, you might need to separate

them to discuss the issue with them individually before bringing them together again.

- *Encourage both sides to listen.* As an emotionally intelligent person, you know that you need to listen. However, most people try to butt in with their counter-arguments without fully listening to each other. If either party tries to talk when they should be listening, take control: "Just a moment, can we hear what he/she has to say first please?" Remembering that your body language can have a greater impact than your words. Use eye contact and nodding to encourage one person to talk at a time.

- *Summarize occasionally what is being said and paraphrase as questions.* This serves a dual purpose. First, it helps to slow the discussion down. When the two parties are firing too much information at each other, they will undoubtedly be unable to take it all in. Second, it forces them to think about what is being said. For example, if one party says, "You shout at me when my work is late, you snipe at me in front of clients, and you never say anything positive about my work," you might summarize and ask a question of the other party by saying, "That's quite a list – how would you respond?" But do not paraphrase all of the time – too much summarizing and paraphrasing will expose your tactic.

- Do not allow either party to attack the other personally. You should allow them to criticize each other's work, but never to criticize each other. So a personal statement such as "You're lazy" should be challenged, but an observation of work quality such as "You've missed the weekly deadline at least twice this month" may be valid.

Playing peacemaker is about helping two parties to listen to each other. It is not about drawing all the attention to yourself by taking absolute control. Let the two parties do most of the talking, and only speak up if you feel that either party is not having a fair opportunity to have their side of the story heard.

Finally, I cannot emphasize enough how crucial it is to remain resolutely impartial throughout. Hold back your own opinions unless you are entitled to speak, because you are their boss. Otherwise, if you take a side – even if that side is clearly right – remember that you will always be on the wrong side for at least one of the parties, and end up creating a new enemy for yourself.

05

Organizational Savvy

We're nearing the end of the book, so let's recap briefly what we've discussed so far. We have discussed self-awareness – paying attention to your emotions and impact on other people. We have talked about self-direction – the ability to manage your moods and emotions to achieve goals. We also covered the third skill of interpersonal savvy – being able to alter the emotions of other people and influence them.

Bringing these skills together, the very pinnacle of emotional intelligence is being able to understand and influence entire teams and organizations as opposed to just single individuals. Being organizationally savvy requires navigating corporate politics, understanding organizational culture, and using both formal and informal channels to achieve your goals.

While emotional intelligence is a skill that ultimately should allow you to realize your own goals, you must always balance your personal goals against those of the organization. If you set out only to further your own goals at the cost of the organization, you will soon be exposed as a self-seeking opportunist. So having organizational savvy is about seeking outcomes that benefit not only yourself but also the organization.

BECOME POLITICALLY AWARE

Office politics gets a bad press. We tend to think of politics as an activity that only scheming, manipulative, self-serving, Machiavellian people engage in. There aren't many positive words associated with office politics. But the truth of the matter is that being alert to political undercurrents is an essential skill for becoming successful. Having an awareness of politics does not mean that you need to behave in an underhand fashion. But being aware of key decision makers and the relationships between them will make your life a lot easier – whether you are aiming to further your personal goals or the greater organizational good.

After all, being able to form rewarding relationships with other people is a useful skill, but it will not help you to achieve your career goals unless you are forming those relationships with the right people.

Begin by looking around your organization for key players. Just as there are people who – if we were being polite – we might describe as a waste of space, there are others who seem to hold undue influence over what goes on in the organization. It is often easy to spot them, as others tend to either like them or respect them (but not necessarily both at the same time). These key players tend to be well connected, so building a relationship with them is often a quick way to build a relationship with the people that they know.

When looking for key players, begin by scrutinizing the people in your own team or department. Not all colleagues are created equal, so who are the more important among them? Key players are not always the named manager or leader of the team or department – so do not fall into the trap of merely looking for the most senior person around. Who are the one or two people that others turn to for help? Who seems to have the most up-to-date news and gossip on what's going on? Once you have spotted them, if you do not already have a strong relationship with them, would it be strategically useful for you to build one?

Another category of useful people is gatekeepers. These individuals may not hold influence in their own right, but they often act as a filter to key players. They are often secretaries, personal assistants, and other support staff whose job it is to block superfluous intrusions into the lives of (typically) senior people. Winning over gatekeepers is often a necessary step to gaining access to the influencer.

Once you have established who the key players and gatekeepers are, the next step is to observe them. Try to find out:

- Who are they each connected with? Look for who they get on well with and seem to have influence over.
- Who do they shun or openly dislike, and why?
- What drives each of these people? If you can identify their innermost needs, you will be able to exert significant influence over them – and in turn, influence the people that they have influence with.

It takes time to develop a full picture of your organization's – or even your team's – politics. But doing so will provide you with invaluable information about how to behave to keep on the right side of the people who matter.

UNDERSTAND YOUR CULTURE

There are times when you may want to break the rules. Yes, there are official rules and regulations, and proscribed processes and procedures that are supposed to dictate how business gets done. But the reality is that behavior is often influenced more by the unofficial culture than official rules.

Culture describes that unwritten set of rules that governs how people should actually behave. The difficulty with culture is that it is intangible – no one ever tells you about it and you can't read up on it – so usually the only time you become aware of these implicit rules is when you break one of them.

Of course you need to respect the hierarchy and official rules of doing business, such as using formal channels to solicit support from other departments. However, people with organizational savvy also grasp the importance of behaving in a culturally appropriate manner.

There are four basic dimensions to culture:

- *Team versus individual performance.* Many organizations claim that they are trying to foster team collaboration, but the reality is that very few manage to do so. For example, I used to work in an organization that claimed that it wanted to promote teamwork between colleagues. However, the fact that it rewarded people with individual sales bonuses meant that it was actually a very individualistic and divisive culture. Knowing whether you should be working selflessly for the benefit of the team or looking after your own interests will ensure you behave in a culturally appropriate manner.

- *High versus low sociability.* In some organizations, people arrive to do their work and then leave at the end of the day, keeping their work lives separate from their personal lives. In other organizations, colleagues go for frequent lunches together and are expected to go drinking in evenings or even on "bonding" weekends together. Identify the sociability of your organization to ensure that you do not overstep boundaries in a low-sociability organization or fail to remain sufficiently visible in a highly sociable organization.

- *Meritocracy versus "politocracy."* Meritocratic organizations vigorously promote the tying of rewards and promotion to performance. For example, if you hit your customer service targets or sales figures for the month, bosses might reward you or at least shower you with plaudits. In other organizations, the actual work you produce is often less important for receiving rewards and promotion than being known and liked by senior managers. Ensure that you focus your efforts on the most important factors – is it the work itself or relationships with key players? – to guarantee your fortune.

- *High versus low risk.* Some organizations encourage people to be creative and take risks, seek new opportunities and create new ventures; others may be very risk averse. However, be careful, as almost every organization claims that it wants to promote creativity and innovation. But remember that what people say about the culture may not actually be how it works. I know, for instance, of an investment bank that says that it is looking for its analysts to take measured risks and seek new opportunities. Indeed, they reward people who take chances and succeed. But the swiftness with which they punish people who take risks and fail shows that the culture is actually incredibly conservative when it comes to taking on risks.

Take a look in your organization at how people work together, socialize together, get promoted, and take risks. Thinking about these four common dimensions of culture, recognize that they should influence not only the behavior of everyone around you but also your behavior. If you do not behave in culturally appropriate ways, you will stick out for all the wrong reasons.

DEEPEN YOUR UNDERSTANDING OF CULTURE

Here is a question for you: what do people wear in your office? You might answer "suits," – but what kind of suits exactly? In one company someone might be able to get away with a suit and shirt from the high street and maybe a polyester/cotton-mix shirt, while in another you might get sneered at unless you are wearing a bespoke suit with a double-cuff shirt with detachable collar stiffeners. At one of my media clients, it seems de rigueur to wear a t-shirt and low-slung jeans to expose an inch of midriff – and that's just the men.

So while the four main dimensions of culture are very important, they by no means tackle all of the unspoken rules about your work.

Apart from dress code (which can assume a huge importance if you do not "fit" your organizational culture), there are all sorts of unwritten rules. Some further considerations for you:

- *How direct are people in their communication – such as making requests and giving each other feedback and criticism?* Just as people in some countries (such as Japan) are less direct than in others (such as the United States and Denmark), employees in certain organizations prefer to be much less direct too. For example, some organizations actively encourage employees to communicate very openly and honestly – seeking their feedback and opinions on a variety of topics. But in other companies, employees know that even when they are being asked for their opinions, being too honest can mark them out as troublemakers. In deciding how honest you can be at work, be careful, as almost all organizations will claim that they welcome opinions.

- *How much control is exerted on employees?* Is your work highly controlled by having to check ideas and plans with your manager, or fill in paperwork and submit budgets for the smallest of projects? Or are you given autonomy and independence to make judgments that you believe are in the best interests of the organization? Overstepping the boundary will get you into trouble, so make sure that you pay attention to how you should be behaving.

- *To what extent does the organization live by its stated values?* Almost all organizations claim to behave with integrity and to treat their employees and customers with respect, yadda, yadda, yadda. But in reality, many companies allow employees to tell "little white lies" to customers or suppliers. If others are breaking the rules to get the job done, you need to either do it too or quit the organization and find one that is more to your liking.

- *What are the unwritten rules about perks and benefits?* Senior managers are usually fairly uptight about official benefits, while middle managers tend to be more relaxed about them, and employees may flout the rules entirely. For example, some companies may allow employees to leave work early or "work from home" occasionally, while others may try to enforce the rules as stipulated in the company handbook. Or one manager may allow an employee to take home a ream of paper for use at home as an unofficial reward for good work – whereas a company director might fire both the manager and employee for disobeying the official rules. Make sure that you respect these rules too.

Deepening your understanding of your culture is a matter of observation and reflection. Look at how the people around you behave, and ask yourself why they behave like that and what you should appear to be doing differently too.

IDENTIFY ROLE MODELS AND MENTORS

When you are at school and you copy someone else's homework, they scold you for it. They call it plagiarizing or stealing. At work it is a different story: Copying more successful people is not only tolerated but actively encouraged. When you spot a practice or behavior that works well and want to learn from it, organizations call it "best practice sharing" or "benchmarking."

The workplace is full of successful people, doing great deeds. If you can spot what it is about them that makes them successful, you can adopt and adapt some of those behaviors to make you more successful too. After all, why reinvent the wheel if you don't have to?

Begin by identifying the most successful people in your organization – the ones who are pretty much universally respected within your organization's culture for certain skills. However, be aware that different people may be role models for different skills. One person could be great at giving presentations but terrible at chairing meetings, while another might be good at negotiating with clients but awful at empathizing with colleagues.

Watch these people in as many different situations as possible, and scrutinize their behavior. What is it that they do or say that makes them respected? Maybe they use their body language in specific ways to make themselves seem more credible or likeable. It could be as simple as the way they introduce themselves to strangers or leave lengthy pauses in conversation to create a feeling of gravitas. Perhaps they have particular turns of phrase that you could borrow for yourself.

Be careful not to copy people wholesale. What works for them may not work for you in exactly the same way. The chief executive may be able to get away with banging a fist on the table during arguments, but then again the chief exec can probably get away with just about anything. The key here is to adopt and *adapt* skills and behaviors to suit you.

Another way to delve even deeper into your organization's culture is to seek a mentor – an experienced individual who you can trust to offer you his or her opinion. Many organizations have mentoring programs in which senior people coach more junior people. But formal programs rarely touch on the really important stuff about understanding culture and politics.

So take it upon yourself to look for a more experienced person that you could approach for advice. Flatter them into mentoring you by explaining that you respect their opinion and want to learn from their greater experience. Then ask why people succeed and fail in the organization. Ask for feedback on your weaknesses. And ask for suggestions on how you could improve your effectiveness and standing within the organization.

Have a think now: Who could you approach to mentor you?

EXERT INDIRECT INFLUENCE

There is nothing more infuriating than trying to persuade someone who is completely unwilling to change their mind. No matter how hard you try to reason with, flatter, or entice them, there are always going to be some people who will remain resolute in denying your request.

When all of your attempts to persuade them have failed, an alternative is to try exerting indirect influence on them through third parties. An individual may not be willing to listen to you, but there must be someone in the organization that they might listen to.

Let's call the person you are trying to influence the "influencee," and the people who you want to exert pressure on them, "influencers."

Use your understanding of the organization's politics to identify people that your target influencee respects. Even the most stubborn of individuals have at least one or two confidants that they trust. Then approach these influencers and position your suggestions as ideas that would ultimately benefit either the influencer or the influencee. Perhaps present it as an opportunity for the influencer to take the credit for your idea – "Our team managed to improve margins by 3 percent last quarter by introducing the new process, but don't tell anyone!"

Or you could try to raise doubts in the influencer's mind – "I hear that our competitor brought in external consultants to revamp their marketing campaign. But I doubt Jonathan would ever let us do anything as radical as that, would he?"

Or show your concern for the influencee – "I can't help but notice that Susan hasn't implemented the new system yet. I hope it doesn't get her into trouble with the senior managers."

Indirect influence is merely a targeted form of peer pressure. When an entire team of people are in favor of an idea, it takes a foolish person to continue to resist it. So the more influencers you can persuade to take your side, the more likely you will be able to change the mind of the influencee.

It takes time and patience to build up a rapport with several influencers, but if the matter is important enough to warrant the effort, you should try it. It works.

DEMONSTRATE INTEGRITY

I have said all along that emotional intelligence is ultimately the art of achieving your personal goals and getting your way with others. But this final section is a warning: There is a fine line between pursuing your goals in a determined fashion and coming across to others as too self-serving. It's the same line that separates influencing others from being seen as manipulating them. And crossing that line could be your undoing.

Integrity is a huge part of behaving with emotional intelligence. Can you remember how it felt the last time someone deceived you, or lied to you, or made you do something that you didn't really want to do? It's the kind of behavior that people usually never forgive or forget.

So in all of your dealings with other people, make sure to balance your personal goals against those of your organization – yes, even if your personal goals have nothing to do with your current organization. For example, you may want to set up your own business, or already have plans to quit and join a competitor. But if you are caught stealing clients, you may get fired and then no one will want to take you on.

When influencing others, weigh up your personal needs against those of others. Again, I know that identifying their hot buttons may allow you to exert a lot of influence on them. But just because you can be assertive does not mean that you always need to be. Learn to back down occasionally – to lose a battle to win the war. If you do not compromise your own needs on occasion and put others first, you will eventually establish yourself as a selfish individual. If you do not reciprocate and demonstrate that you have their best interests at heart as well, they will feel used and manipulated.

Always weigh up the consequences of your actions. When following your personal goals and influencing others to achieve your goals, keep in mind the goals of your organization and the needs of others too. If you don't get that balance right, you can imagine the damage it will inflict on not only your relationships with people but also ultimately your career.

It's okay to think dark thoughts about your personal goals and how you want to manipulate others into doing your bidding. But always behave towards people with integrity. Or at least make sure that you never get caught!

About the Author

Dr Rob Yeung is a director at leading business psyhology consultancy Talentspace, where he specialize in interviewing and assessing senior managers. He also coaches executives, particularly in the areas of leadership and charisma. He works with a wide range of organizations including investment banks, law and accountancy firms, airlines, and advertising and media business.

He has written nine books on management topics and is often asked to contribute to print media including the *Guardian* and *Financial Times* as well as broadcast media including CNN.

A business school lecturer and frequently requested conference speaker, he is also the presenter of a highly acclaimed BBC television series on job hunting.